IMAGES
of America

AROUND CAROGA LAKE, CANADA LAKE, AND PINE LAKE

The lake community of Caroga Lake, Canada Lake, and Pine Lake lies in the northern portion of Fulton County, New York, which is home to 44 lakes. Approximately half of the county's lakes are in or near the subject area for this book. Surrounding the lakes are mature forests, from which businesses grew, hotels were constructed, lake cottages were built, and amusement parks sprouted. (Courtesy of Richard and Judy Arthur.)

ON THE COVER: Early in the 20th century, East Caroga Lake and West Caroga Lake meet under the bridge. In 1938, the channel was deepened to allow passage of motorboats from one lake to the other, and this process was repeated in 1969.

IMAGES
of America

AROUND CAROGA LAKE, CANADA LAKE, AND PINE LAKE

Carol Parenzan Smalley
Foreword by Peter Betz

ARCADIA
PUBLISHING

Published by Arcadia Publishing
Charleston, South Carolina

Library of Congress Control Number: 2010940123

For all general information, please contact Arcadia Publishing:
Telephone 843-853-2070
Fax 843-853-0044
E-mail sales@arcadiapublishing.com
For customer service and orders:
Toll-Free 1-888-313-2665

Visit us on the Internet at www.arcadiapublishing.com

*This book is dedicated to Barbara McMartin (1931–2005),
whose vision for her Adirondack home will forever shape
the mountainous landscape of six million acres.*

CONTENTS

FOREWORD

Numerous examples, dating from the latter half of the 19th century, exist of the rapid commercial rise, temporary success, and sudden demise of small Adirondack one-industry villages. The history of Wheelerville, at the inlet to Canada Lake, and its once-dominant Wheeler-Claflin Company illustrates a typical boom-to-bust situation, one in which an almost unspoiled forest community, occupied by but a handful of farmers and smallish lumber mills, is also blessed by possessing an abundance of at least one easily accessed natural product. Surrounding Wheelerville, acres of hemlock trees, an essential component in the process of leather tanning, abounded.

Neither William Claflin, the owner of large shoe factories near Boston, nor Jonathan Wheeler was a "local boy." They were unemotional businessmen from Massachusetts seeking large quantities of tannic acid—obtained from the bark of hemlock trees—to produce leather for their shoes. During the mid-1860s, the Wheeler-Claflin interests bought 20,000 acres of hemlocks to process. Lumber mills followed the tanning mills, since all tanners wanted from hemlock trees was bark. Hotels, boardinghouses, and taverns sprang up in the newly minted village of Wheelerville to house, feed, and quench the thirst of lumbermen and tannery workers, all of whom were enjoying the generous pay rate approaching $2 per day.

For approximately 25 years (1865–1890), residents of Wheelerville and the town of Caroga reaped a good economic harvest from Wheeler-Claflin's tanning and lumbering activities, but when their 20,000 acres of hemlock trees were exhausted, the tannery closed. The Wheeler-Claflin Company and its workforce of tanners moved elsewhere; no longer were there steady incomes to be reaped by local Wheelerville residents in providing ancillary services, such as room and board, laundering, blacksmithing to repair tools, and so on.

The Wheelerville Store closed in 1893, but Wheelerville did not become a ghost town. It retained its identity, partly because the Caroga Town Offices continued there, as did educational and religious institutions. However the village's economic progress, in spite of the 1918–1929 presence of the Holden Lumber Company sawmill, never resumed momentum. Summer lakeside camps now dot the sides of Caroga, Canada, and Pine Lakes, where old-time tanyards, lumber mills, and millponds once flourished.

—Peter Betz
Fulton County historian

ACKNOWLEDGMENTS

With heartfelt gratitude for sharing stories, photographs, and Adirondack memories with me, I thank the following: Adirondack Museum, Richard and Judith Arthur, Marion Bayly, Thomas Bergami, Dan Berggren, Peter Betz (Fulton County historian), Arthur and Jane Bornt, Marion "Bonnie" Yates Buchner, Caroga Fish and Game Club, Caroga Historical Association and Museum, Bart Carrig, Laurence D'Alessandris, Dona Dise, Barbara Donnelly, Anthony and Kathleen Ermie, Mark "Buzz" Van Etters, Linda Fake, Robert Fear, Shirley Florczyk, Fulton County Museum, Fulton County Regional Chamber of Commerce and Industry, Fulton-Montgomery Community College, Linda Gilbert, Glove Theatre and Museum, Donald and Gerd Curtis, David and Catherine Graves, Dorianne Gray, Jerry and Kim Groom, Richard and Mary Groshans, Robert and Patricia Hagen, Anna Marie Hansel, George and Shirley Holliday, Donald and Erma Hoffman, Larry Holmes, Jeffrey Houck, William and Chardel Houck, John Ivancic, John Ivancic Jr., Kenneth Jackson, Johnstown Historical Association, Johnstown Public Library, William Kitchen, Kyna Kuhlman, Leroy and Betty Lane, the *Leader-Herald*, William and Joan Loveday, Inger McDaniel (historian for the Town of Caroga), Michael Manning, Mohawk Valley Library System, Patricia Moran, New York State Department of Environmental Conservation, North Bush Methodist Church, North-South Skirmish Association, Darla Oathout, Cathy Ossenfort, Dale Parmer, Raymond and Jean Parnell, Margaret Reaney Memorial Library (St. Johnsville), Colleen Ricciardi, Joseph Ricciardi, Karen Riley, Susan Rokos, Jeannine Schwartz, Wayne and Nancy Seeley, Janet Sherman Shepard, Douglas and Judith Smith, Southern Adirondack Library System, Barbara Spraker, Charles and Lois Svehla, Town of Caroga, Margaret Western, and Donald Williams. Thank you to Rebekah Mower and Erin Rocha of Arcadia Publishing for their endless patience. For those I failed to list, I apologize. Thank you.

A special thank you to everyone who welcomed my family to this area years ago and for making us feel at home in the mountains. One final thanks goes to my summer friends at Pine Lake for saving me a corner of the sand on those glorious summer days. May you continue to hear the voice of the loon—the "Song of the Wilderness."

INTRODUCTION

Along the southern border, or Blue Line, of the Adirondack Park in Upstate New York lie Caroga Lake, Canada Lake, and Pine Lake. These three lakes, plus about a dozen more, form the town of Caroga. At one time, their fertile fishing grounds enticed Native Americans, early explorers, and Adirondack guides to this Fulton County community. The mature woods that surrounded the lakes attracted the logging and tanning industries. Amusement parks, grand hotels, and dance halls drew crowds from nearby towns and far away. Artists came to find inspiration and left behind their creative marks.

An Adirondack guide, who became legend, once walked these lands. Nicholas "Nick" Stoner called Caroga Lake area his home. Local politicians immortalized the veteran of two wars and master trapper and hunter. Today, Stoner's name is embedded into the name of the golf course, an island, two lakes, and an inn.

It was along the bank of West Caroga Lake that Frank Sherman built his amusement park around 1920. His vision would last for more than 50 years. Today, the skeletal remains of the dance hall, carousel house, arcade, and Ferris wheel anxiously await a new owner with a fresh vision.

Artists, writers, and filmmakers summered on Canada Lake in the early 1900s. They would work diligently during the day and party with wild abandon at night. Today's children still enjoy books that were created by some of these artists as they worked in their lakeside studios.

Joseph Groshans built a dance hall and large beach at Pine Lake in the mid-1920s. An amusement park sprouted then wilted away. Property changed hands numerous times, as one person's misfortune allowed for another's fortune. Today, that dance hall and beach still draw summer crowds.

Summer people bought inexpensive plots of logged land on and around the lakes to build summer cottages and camps. Logs were drifted across the lakes and made into seasonal homes. Like much of the country, the lake area has watched real estate values rise only to plummet. The area is currently experiencing new growth.

It was not easy to reach these North Woods. Trains would transport travelers to nearby Fonda, about 16 miles away, and from there, visitors traveled by way of carriage service or coach on old plank roads. Steamers collected passengers at the outlet and carried them across Canada Lake to grand hotels and clubs. Ladies in their Sunday finest would row across the lake to dance the night away to the sounds of big bands, only to return at the end of the night by the light of lanterns. The automobile would make the journey to the lakes easier. Cars packed the parking areas and blocked the roads leading north. New roads and bridges were built. The lakes were the place to be for summer fun.

Famous people found their way to the lake community. Atop a hill, overlooking the lakes, lived one family who owned several elaborate hotels and movie houses. Here, secret guests would slip in and out during the night, unbeknownst to those who slept below. One presidential family came to visit the area and left a precious item behind on a lake bottom. A gangster stopped one evening for dinner. And some not so famous people made their mark as well. Like most mountain communities, the lakes were also home to those who sought solitude.

In all this grandeur, there were challenges. The tanning industry stripped the mountains of their most precious resource, leaving behind bare logs and lake pollution. Many of those bare logs were milled and used to build the community's next chapter. It would take years for the second growth forest to establish itself, due in part to the oversight of the Adirondack Park Agency, which manages six million acres of privately and publicly owned Upstate New York wilderness, and the advocacy of one Canada Lake resident, who received numerous state appointments, recognitions, and honors for her relentless campaign to keep the mountains "forever wild."

Grand hotels were planned and built, only to be lost to aggressive fires, then built again. Today, there are no grand hotels, only grand ideas. Businesses were started, with some owners filing bankruptcy, more than once. But perseverance won, and the lakes overflowed with entrepreneurial spirit. Relentless winter months would test the fortitude of those who called the lakes their home. Lake ice would form early and leave late, making travel around the lakes difficult. Snow fell not in inches but feet. Flooding conditions threatened the dams that formed the lakes. Dams broke and were rebuilt.

The challenges offered opportunity, however. The "wildness" brought those with an adventurous spirit to ski at a new downhill ski area, to ride endless miles of snowmobile trails, to hike to mountain peaks and hidden lakes, and to fish and hunt. Ice was harvested from the lakes not only to keep food cool in the summer but also to build toboggan runs down mountainsides in the winter. Where steamboats once traveled, sailboats and motorboats now cruised. Buildings that were no longer needed were repurposed with new intent. Cleared land was earmarked for recreation.

From a small lumbering community tucked within the Adirondack Mountains, the town of Caroga grew. Although some industries and businesses prospered then dissipated, others have survived the challenging times, and the spirit of the people continues to reside along the shores of these lakes. Today's lakes are pristine, with little evidence of past abuses. New four-season and summer homes are being constructed. Today, these lakes attract full-time residents, seasonal camp and cottage owners, and visiting guests. Generations of families carry on tradition as they camp, swim, watch fireworks, and await once more the music of the carousel and the smell of the famous yellow popcorn.

Arts and culture thrive within the community. A museum spotlighting life in a southern Adirondack community welcomes visitors, hosts artist exhibits, and conducts workshops for children and adults. Music glides over the water again as Adirondack folksingers perform on the museum grounds. And, on the water itself, live the loons, a symbol of this Adirondack community. Summer comes and goes with its vocal cries and glorious dancing.

The community can never be what it once was. But those times can be the foundation for what it has the potential to become. Trees came down, and buildings went up. Tanned hides and lumber traveled south below, while visitors ventured north above. Although the steamers may no longer blast their whistles across the lake, one thing still remains the same—the water still calls all who will listen.

One

A LUMBERING COMMUNITY

The following is from J.H. French's 1860 *Gazetteer of the State of New York*: "Caroga was formed from the towns of Stratford, Bleeker, and Johnstown April 11, 1842. Its surface is rolling in the south and broken in the north by small, sharp mountains. Numerous clusters of lakes lie in the center and north part of town. A small portion of the area only is susceptible of cultivation. Lumbering is the principal business." (Courtesy of the Town of Caroga.)

The three main lakes in the town of Caroga are Caroga Lake (West and East), Canada Lake, and Pine Lake. Caroga Lake was originally called Garoga Lake. The creek that flowed south from its outlet, however, was Caroga Creek. Canada Lake was once called East Fish Lake, East Canada Lake, or Byrn Lake. Pine Lake has always been called Pine Lake. Other lakes—Green Lake, Otter Lake, Lily Lake, West Lake, Mud Lake, Nine Corner Lake, and the Stoner Lakes—surround these three. The map shown was generated from surveys by B. Nichols and was first published in 1868. (Courtesy of the Town of Caroga.)

12

In the mid-1830s, Garrett A. Newkirk settled in what became Newkirks Mills. To operate a sawmill, Newkirk built a small dam on Caroga Creek. The first tannery for the area was also located here. Built in 1843 by Newkirk and John Littlejohn, the tannery was operated by Lewis Rider for two years. Seen in the background of this photograph is the Dutch Reformed Church. (Courtesy of the Town of Caroga.)

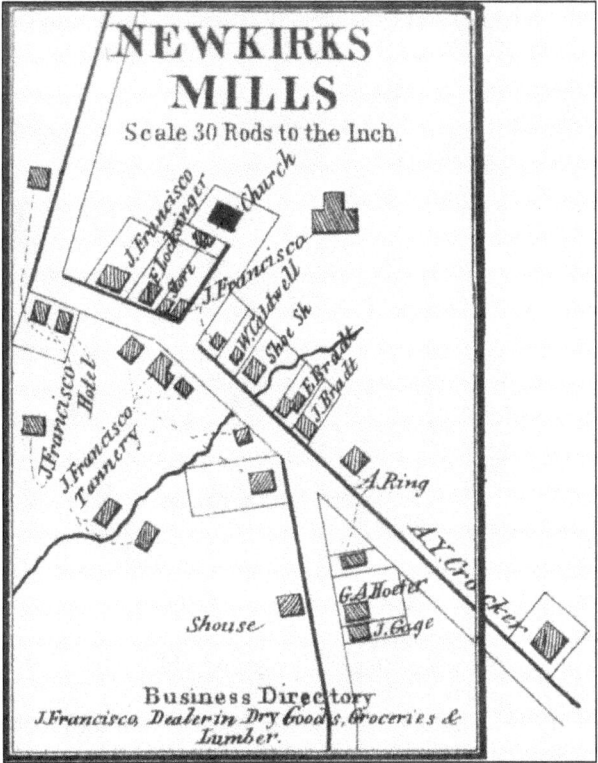

Although first called McEwens Corners because of McEwen's Gristmill being located there, the community of Newkirks Mills expanded rapidly. Located along the banks of the Caroga Creek near the lake's outlet, it grew to include a Dutch Reformed Church, schoolhouse, store, post office, sawmill, tannery, and homesteads. Garrett A. Newkirk, founder of the community, served as its postmaster from 1839 to 1858. (Courtesy of the Town of Caroga.)

13

Trees were lumbered and sent to area mills to make wood products, such as broom and mop handles. At the time of this 1950 photograph, the community of Newkirks Mills had been lumbering for over 100 years. Here, independent logger Tunis Lane (center) and his two sons, Harold (left) and Milton (right), work the land. (Courtesy of Leroy and Betty Lane.)

The weather was both a challenge and a blessing to the pioneers of the lake area. An abundance of snow over frozen ground made it easier to log the land. Horses would pull skidders with logs to either a landing site or directly to the mill for processing. Here, horses rest in front of the Auskerada Hotel. (Courtesy of the Town of Caroga.)

OLD NEWKIRKS DAY

Garrett A. Newkirk Mansion

A Bicentennial Program

TO COMMEMORATE THE FOUNDING OF THE
TOWN OF CAROGA IN 1842

and

TO DEDICATE A HISTORICAL MARKER
DESIGNATING THE LAST HOME OF
MAJOR NICHOLAS STONER

Newkirks, New York

August 15, 1976

While the nation celebrated its bicentennial, the town of Caroga celebrated its 200th birthday in 1976. Although the North Bush area was probably the first to be settled in the area, Newkirks Mills was the location of the first meeting of town officials in 1842 when the town was established. The inaugural gathering for the town of Caroga was held at the home of Garrett A. Newkirk, who was elected the first town supervisor. Almost 130 years later, the town would have its first woman chairman, Emma Krause, elected in 1971. On July 4, 1976, all the church bells in the town were rung in celebration of both the nation and the town. One month later, the town hosted walking tours of Newkirks Mills and dedicated a state historic marker at the last home of Nicholas Stoner, which still sits along Route 10, just south of Caroga Lake. (Courtesy of the Town of Caroga.)

Although historians agree that this building is from the Newkirks Mills area from the mid-1800s, they are uncertain as to its function. This structure by the creek may have been a cheese factory. Note the arch under the bridge. At the top center of the arch is a keystone, or wedge-shaped object, that holds the structure together. A wooden frame was built first to position the stones, then removed. (Courtesy of the Town of Caroga.)

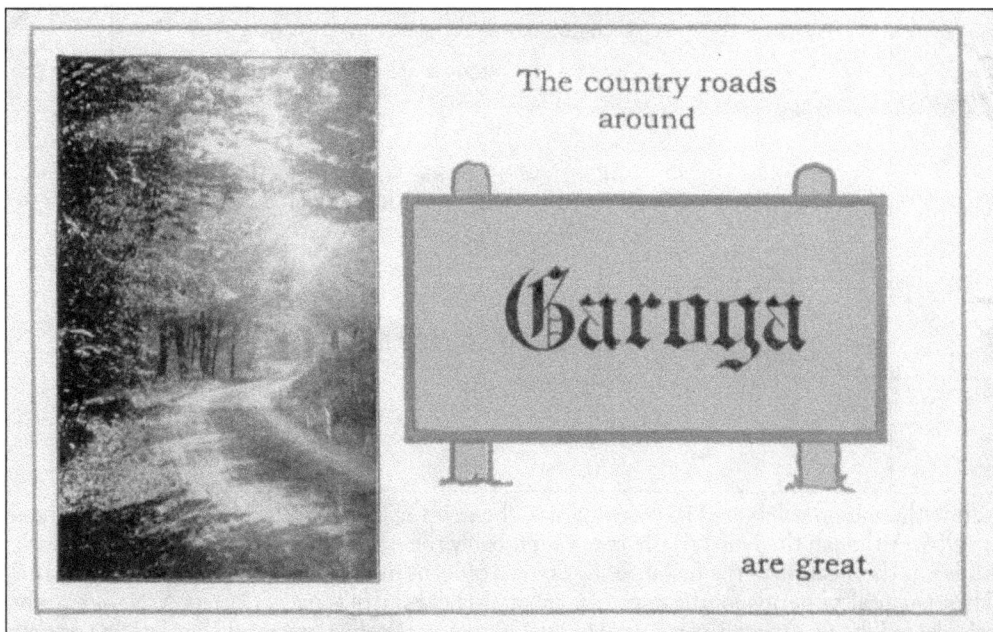

The country roads around

Garoga

are great.

Is it Caroga or Garoga? The word *Caroga* is a Native American word, meaning "by the streams or waterways." Most of the earlier maps and references of the area denoted Garoga Lake and Caroga Creek. Today, it is Caroga Lake and the town of Caroga. The name Garoga is still used to denote an area along the creek, south of the town of Caroga. (Courtesy of David and Catherine Graves.)

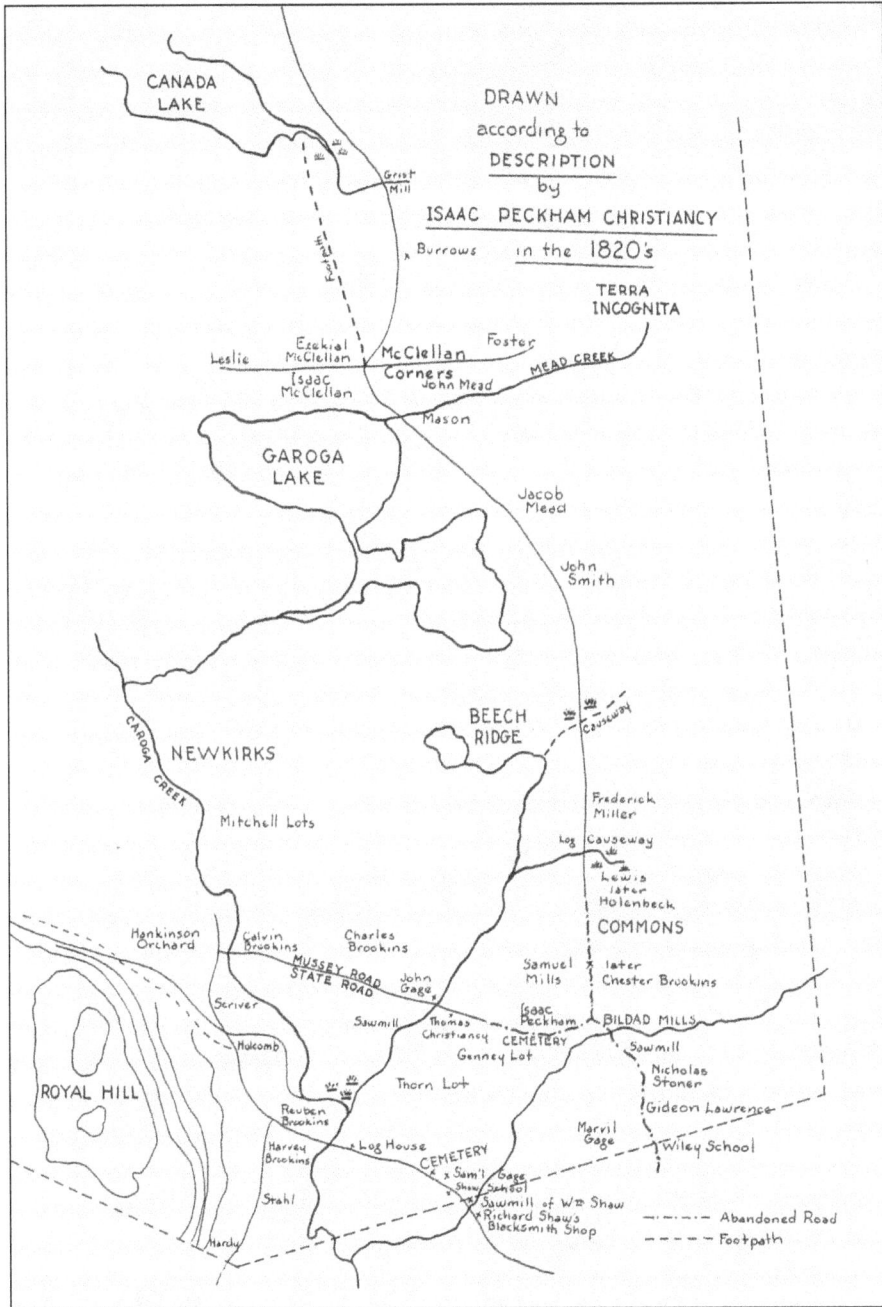

CANADA LAKE

DRAWN
according to
DESCRIPTION
by
ISAAC PECKHAM CHRISTIANCY
in the 1820's

TERRA
INCOGNITA

Grist
Mill

Footpath

Burrows

Leslie

Ezekial
McClellam

Isaac
McClellan

McClellan
Corners

Foster

John Mead

MEAD CREEK

Mason

GAROGA
LAKE

Jacob
Mead

John
Smith

BEECH
RIDGE

Causeway

CAROGA CREEK

NEWKIRKS

Mitchell Lots

Frederick
Miller

Log Causeway

Lewis
later
Holenbeck

COMMONS

Hankinson
Orchard

Calvin
Brookins

Charles
Brookins

Samuel
Mills

later
Chester Brookins

MUSSEY ROAD
STATE ROAD

John
Gage

Scriver

Sawmill

Thomas
Christiancy

Isaac
Peckham

BILDAD MILLS

Sawmill

Holcomb

CEMETERY

Genney Lot

Nicholas
Stoner

Gideon Lawrence

ROYAL HILL

Reuben
Brookins

Thorn Lot

Marvil
Gage

Wiley School

Harvey
Brookins

Log House

CEMETERY

Sam'l Gage
Shaw School

Stahl

Sawmill of Wm Shaw
Richard Shaws
Blacksmith Shop

Hardy

Abandoned Road
Footpath

This is a map drawn in the 1820s by Isaac Peckham Christiancy, one of the area's earliest settlers and a founder of the Grand Old Party (GOP). Note the cluster of homesteads, businesses, and schools in the southern section. New settlers moved in from the south, primarily from the Johnstown area, expanding northward as they followed the creeks to their headwaters. Christiancy was born in 1812 in a log home in the North Bush area. Christiancy moved from Upstate New York to Michigan in 1833, where he became a lawyer, judge, and US senator. He returned to North Bush in 1875 to visit his boyhood home. He died in 1890 in Michigan. (Courtesy of the Town of Caroga.)

Prior to the year 1752, the Mohawk Indians were in undisputed possession of all the territory embraced within the boundaries of the Town of Caroga. The agricultural lands cultivated by the Mohawks were on the lower reaches of the Caiohoran Creek, the Indian name of the outlet of Canada Lake, of the Garoga Creek and of the Cayadutta Creek, along which streams the remains of very extensive villages exist, and also on the Mohawk River where their fortified towns were located after intercommunication with white men had commenced.

Soon after the Dutch settled at Albany traders from among them penetrated the Mohawk country. They invariably visited only the Mohawk River castles of the Indians and wrote only concerning what they saw. Those writings therefor describe the Indian castles on the Mohawk only and do not mention the settlements elsewhere. Judging from the remains that have been found since the passage of the Indians, two most populous Mohawk towns were located, one on the Cayadutta near Samsonsville, the other on the Garoga below the present hamlet of Garoga. These may have been the towns that antedated the Mohawk occupation of this section but that they were Mohawk towns is proven by the multitude of trade relics found in both those places.

There were in this town, however, three village sites occupied by them--possibly only for convenience in hunting and fishing. The country about must have been at that time a hunters' and fishermen's paradise. The sites were located just north of West Caroga Lake on the flat land adjoining the lake, on the flat land separating West Canada and Canada Lakes at the outlet of those lakes, and another one on the shore of Stoner Lake in the northern part of the town.

Cyrus Durey wrote a history of the area around 1920, in which he stated that prior to 1752, Mohawks were in possession of this land. Three Native American settlements were known to exist—one between the two Caroga Lakes, one between Canada and West Lakes, and the other near Stink Lakes, later called Stoner Lakes. The Mohawk Indians were, and continue to be, part of the Iroquois Nation. Native American paths crossed through the region. The Old Indian Path, which crossed through an area south of Newkirks Mills called Glasgow, would become an official road in 1796. The Glasgow Road led to a millpond and mill wheel operated by waterpower. At this site, clothespins, wagon spokes, and handles for brooms and mops were made. The lumbering operation at Glasgow ended in 1898. (Courtesy of the Town of Caroga.)

CENSUS SCHEDULE

TO BE KEPT IN THE REGISTER

Names of parents or other persons with whom the children live	NAMES AND DATES OF BIRTH OF CHILDREN BETWEEN 5 AND 18 (Follow the form given below) Census of August 30, 1925 Use a line for each name; when space is not sufficient the names of children in the same family may be placed on one line as follows:	Children between 5 and 18	
		Male	Female
(Example) J. Richards	James, Aug. 20, 1912 Charles, July 15, 1914 Ellen, May 7, 1916	2	1
George Bowers	Anthony, Sept. 10, 1908; John, Nov. 5, 1915	4	1
" "	Marian, Feb. 22, 1910; Paul, Jan. 15, 1912		
" "	George, Sept. 8, 1912.		
George Chappell	Edna, Sept. 12, 1907; Lyman, July 18, 1915	2	1
" "	Floyd, May 23, 1911.		
Guy Lurey	Dorothy, Nov. 17, 1907		1
Burtell Foster	Harry, Feb. 11, 1908; Wesley, Jan. 10, 1912	3	1
" "	Edith, Mar. 22, 1910; Chester, Aug. 23, 1915		
Jerome Foster	George, Sept. 4, 1915	1	
Elmer Martin	Wilmer, Aug. 13, 1910	1	
George McWalter	Florence, June 27, 1918; Geneive, June 23, 1915	2	2
" "	Raymond, Aug. 30, 1911.		
" "	Lawrence, Sept. 25, 1908		
Sam Sandford	Alta, Aug. 6, 1918; Thelma, Jan. 18, 1912		2
Michael Schmitz	Albertina, Jan. 31, 1910.	1	1
" "	Michael, July 12, 1913.		
Conrad Shutts	Edna, Nov. 29, 1908; Clayton, Mar. 29, 1907	2	1
" "	Edward, Oct. 12, 1910.		
De Forest Bullard	De Forest, Dec. 15, 1915; Hilda, Jan 13, 1919	1	2
" "	Margarite, July 24, 1914		
Ward Nixon	Ward, July 15, 1920.	1	
Harry Hough	Joseph, May 18, 1910; Dorothy, Aug. 2, 1912	1	1
Mabel Lurey	Jack —	1	
		20	13

This 1925–1926 census shows 20 males and 13 females attending one of the schools located in the lake region. In 1845, only 342 people resided in the town of Caroga (which includes the three main lakes). Of the 342 people, only 79 of them were farmers. By 1855, almost 700 people resided in the area, with most of this growth due to the lumber industry. To transport lumber to the railroad in Fonda, a plank road was built in 1849, connecting Newkirks Mills to the river town below. This plank road would later be extended to accommodate the flow of business traffic at the Wheelerville Tannery and beyond. Today, about 1,500 people are considered full-time residents of the area. The population, however, multiplies during the summer months, when camps and cottages are opened for the warm-weather months. (Courtesy of the Town of Caroga.)

New York Roll.

(No. 1695.)

Nicholas Stoner, 4

Private

New York line — 1777 6 years

In the army of the United States during the Revolutionary War

Inscribed on the Roll of New York

at the rate of 8 Dollars per month, to commence on

the 8th of April 1818.

Certificate of Pension issued the 30. of June 1818,

and sent to the Pensioner at

Johnstown, New York.

Arrears to 4th of Sept. 1818.

4 months 27/30. $ 39.20

Revolutionary claim,
Act 18th March, 1818.

Van calland

Town Unknown Montgomery Co.

Having fought in the Revolutionary War and the War of 1812, Caroga native Nicholas Stoner applied for and received a military pension in 1818, equal to $8 a month. Stoner's efforts as a soldier, woodsman, trapper, and hunter was memorialized in *Trappers of New York* by Jeptha Root Simms, published in 1850, in which he wrote the following about Stoner's life in 1846: "An old trapper resides in the town of Garoga, Fulton County; at a settlement which has recently sprung up, called Newkirk's Mills. He owns a comfortable dwelling in which he lives, (and) draws a pension from the general government . . . is situated pleasantly on the outlet of Garoga Lakes, two crystal sheets of water." James Fenimore Cooper modeled the main character in his book, *The Deerslayer*, after this Caroga legend. Stoner's home was recognized in 1976 with a New York State historic marker. (Courtesy of the Town of Caroga.)

To commemorate the contributions of Nicholas "Nick" Stoner, the people of Fulton County purchased war bonds between January 18 and February 15, 1944. The SS *Nick Stoner*, with hull number 2307, was officially launched on June 17, 1944, and scrapped in 1964. This marker, honoring an influential Caroga Lake resident, sits before the Fulton County Courthouse in Johnstown. (Courtesy of Johnstown Historical Society.)

THIS LIBERTY SHIP
NICK STONER
SPONSORED AND MADE POSSIBLE
BY THE WAR BOND PURCHASES
OF THE PEOPLE OF
FULTON COUNTY
NEW YORK
JANUARY 18, 1944 – FEBRUARY 15, 1944

The residents of the area celebrated the life of Nick Stoner on July 24, 1982. To recognize the lake legend, soldier, and Adirondack guide, a monument of Stoner sits atop the Nick Stoner Golf Course, seen here. The bronze statue was dedicated on August 21, 1929. Some attending the dedication ceremony thought that statue reminded them of Michelangelo's David. Stoner died November 24, 1853, at the age of 92. (Courtesy of Caroga Historical Association and Museum.)

With these words, "the lands now or hereafter constituting the Forest Preserve shall be forever kept as wild forest lands," the Adirondack Forest Preserve was created in 1885. The Adirondack Park was formed in 1892 and includes both private and public lands totaling almost six million acres. The lake area sits in the Ferris Lake Wild Forest Preserve, along the southern Blue Line, or boundary. (Courtesy of Janet Sherman Shepard.)

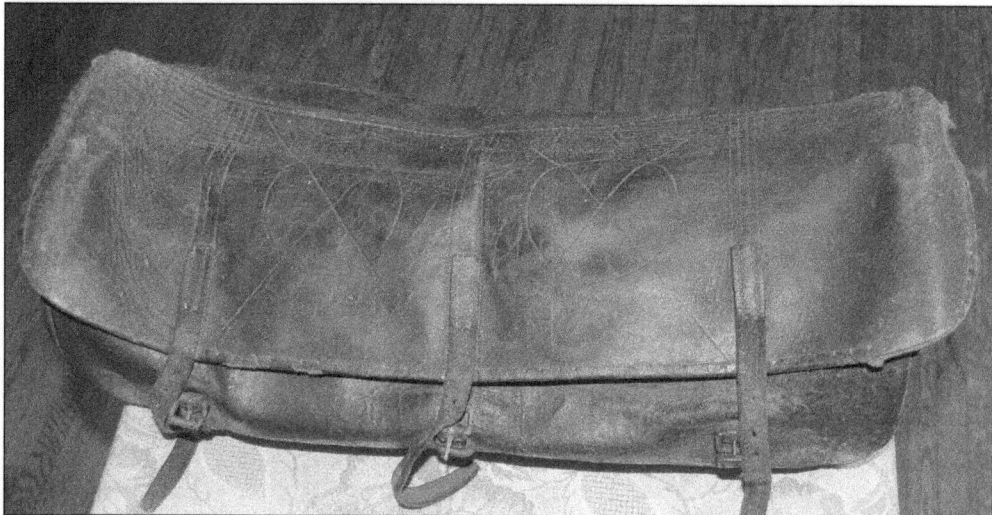

The climate of the town of Caroga changed abruptly in the 1860s when Massachusetts-based William Claflin arrived in the upstate forest community with this valise. With Jonathan Wheeler, he purchased 20,000 acres of mature forest for less than $4 an acre and logged and debarked the hemlock trees for their tannin to cure leather for his shoe-manufacturing business. In 1890, he departed the area, leaving his worn leather bag behind. (Courtesy of Johnstown Historical Society.)

Two

CAROGA LAKE

Caroga Lake consists of two lakes, East Caroga Lake and West Caroga Lake. Along West Caroga Lake "stood" Old Guard. This leaning pine welcomed those who passed by on Shore Road. After witnessing fireworks over the lake on many a Fourth of July and dives off the top of the platform, it fell to the water in the 1960s. It leaned until it could lean no more. (Courtesy of Donald and Erma Hoffman.)

This Indenture,

In the late 1890s and early 1900s, land along the lakeshores was purchased to build summer camps. This deed shows the transfer of South Shore land from landowners Frank and Elizabeth Groshans to Andrew H. Witze, a pharmacist from Brooklyn, for $100. Andrew and his wife, Elizabeth, built Camp Elizabeth along East Caroga Lake by floating oak trees across the water. To reach camp, the Witzes would take a train from Brooklyn to Fonda, where they would transfer to a horse-drawn carriage for the remainder of their travels. Family members would row to Sherman's Park at night to attend dances, returning by lantern light. Today, the camp is still owned by five of the Witze family members. (Both, courtesy of Arthur and Jane Bornt.)

The evolution of the Knight's Store in Caroga represented the changing lake community. This photograph is of the store in 1910, after about 10 years of operation, and shows the first of several additions. Notice the telephone sign. The store would continue to grow and, eventually, would become the residence of Holton Seeley, the area's forest ranger. (Courtesy of David and Catherine Graves.)

Automobiles made travel around the lakes easier. Here, a car navigates along the shore of West Caroga Lake on a primitive dirt road. Some of the dirt roads in the area were covered with macadam in the mid-1910s, making the trip quicker and less dusty. (Courtesy of Caroga Historical Association and Museum.)

The boathouse, known as Simonson's Point, was developed around 1905. Using one of the few generators in the area, the boathouse was lit most nights. Church services were held in the boathouse on Sundays, and the Simonsons hosted regattas, water races, and other activities for nearby camp residents. Electricity would come to Caroga Lake in 1925. A rustic footbridge extended from the Simonsons' farmhouse to a stand of pine trees, known as Whitman's Point or Pine Point. A footpath extended around the entire lake, and on Sunday afternoons, residents would walk around the lake. In 1947, a devastating tornado ripped through the area, downing numerous trees and causing widespread destruction of the lake area. (Courtesy of Caroga Historical Association and Museum.)

This group of boaters and bathers gathered on West Caroga Lake in the early 1910s for an afternoon of fun in the Caroga sun. Notice that the women are attired in long "swim dresses" or Sunday best outfits and that there is a chair back attached to a seat for comfort in one of the rowboats! (Courtesy of Caroga Historical Association and Museum.)

Many of the camps along Caroga Lake were built on points, or protrusions, and could be reached only by boat. An example of this is Breezy Point, built around 1900. To protect these camps and the lakes they sat on from rapid growth, the Caroga Lake Protective Association was formed about the same time this camp was built. Camp owners could participate through association membership. (Courtesy of Caroga Historical Association and Museum.)

One of the most popular activities at Caroga Lake in the early 1920s was swimming. Here, sitting along the pier at Sherman's Park on West Caroga Lake, is a group of water enthusiasts. In the summer of 1921, new excitement came to the lake. Throughout the previous year, Frank Sherman built bathhouses, a two-story pavilion, and a dance hall. Some consider Sherman the "Walt Disney" of Caroga Lake. (Courtesy of Donald and Erma Hoffman.)

Better known as the "Rooster" for his early morning crows on the lake, Pearley Howard lived a reclusive life on Alderwood Park Road. Feeling a bit lonely one summer, he advertised for a wife. A prospect arrived to find that Rooster owned only one knife, one fork, and one spoon. She departed quickly. Sharing the log with the Rooster (center) are Barbara Kowalski (left) and William Kowalski (right). (Courtesy of Barbara Donnelly.)

Flooding has always been a concern in this water-based community. Here, in the late 1930s, water overtook Sherman's Park. Fire caused significant damage in 1979, enough to require the sale of the original wooden carousel animals to create restoration funds. One of the sold animals now resides in the Carousel Museum at Knoebels Amusement Resort in Elysburg, Pennsylvania. Currently the property is for sale. (Courtesy of Janet Sherman Shepard.)

Prompted by past fires that caused destruction, Charles Putnam, town supervisor, encouraged the formation and incorporation of the Caroga Lake Volunteer Fire Company, Inc., in 1951. Not everyone was in favor of a new vehicle, however. Emma Krause, future town supervisor, was heard to say the following: "There goes Charlie with his milk truck. He is going to milk the taxpayers with it." In 2002, Barbara DeLuca became its first female fire chief. (Courtesy of the Town of Caroga.)

A trip to Caroga Lake and Sherman's Park was not complete without a taste of its famous yellow popcorn. The popcorn became a signature product for the park. Some people believed they knew it was summer when they could smell the popcorn miles away down in town. In the picture below, Trixie, a monkey who perched high above the crowds, often greeted visitors to Sherman's Park on West Caroga Lake in the 1930s. Trixie was one of the first "snowbirds" to summer at Caroga and winter in Florida. Each fall, Joseph and Elizabeth Sherman would place Trixie on a southbound train to enjoy the winter sunshine before returning the following spring. It is believed that Trixie was quite fond of peanuts soaked in beer. (Left, courtesy of Caroga Historical Association and Museum; below, courtesy of Janet Sherman Shepard.)

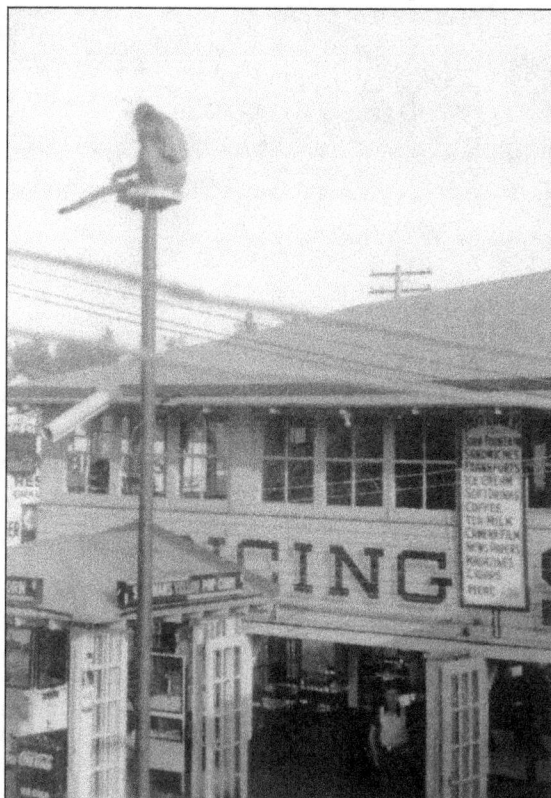

Three

CANADA LAKE

Canada Lake

THIS LAKE is sixteen hundred and fifty feet above tide water in the most southerly spur of the Adirondacks. The largest of a cluster of fifteen lakes within a radius of six miles, all of which are nestled among mountains of virgin wilderness, the haunt of fish and deer, and all accessible by carriage road, boat or trail. There is no prettier sheet of water in the whole Adirondack region than Canada Lake, and the steamer trip to Stewart's Dam, 8 miles away, is even more charming than the famous Songo River in Maine.

Each succeeding year city people find the most potential tonic for wrecked nerves among the lakes and mountains, and a month or two spent here each summer carries with it a longer lease on life.

The "pretty sheet of water" attracted wealthy travelers. This Auskerada marketing brochure from around 1900 stated that Canada Lake is "the largest of a cluster of fifteen lakes within a radius of six miles" and that "city people find the most potential tonic for wrecked nerves among the lakes and mountains, and a month or two spent here each summer carries with it a longer lease on life." (Courtesy of David and Catherine Graves.)

Rough Point, a private camp on Kasson Drive, was built around 1894 for Albert and Frances Simmons. The land was originally owned by William and Mary B. Claflin, who sold it to J.H. Decker, a wealthy Johnstown glove manufacturer, with the specification that the building cost "at least four hundred dollars and be covered with a coat of paint." Today, William and Joan Loveday own the camp. (Courtesy of William and Joan Loveday.)

At the end of the 19th century and the beginning of the 20th century, travel on Canada Lake was often by steamer. The first ship on the lake was *Water Lily*, sailing in the 1870s and 1880s. Other steamers included *Wanderer*, *Whip-poor-will*, *Kanaughta*, *Auskerada*, and *Bedbug*. Several dives have been made in Canada Lake to search for remains of steamboats. To date, none have been found. (Courtesy of Richard and Judy Arthur.)

Auskerada Hotel, Canada Lake, N. Y.

As part of a developing summer resort push in the late 1890s and early 1900s, the Auskerada was built in 1893 on the site of the old Canada Lake House, which had succumbed to fire in 1884. The four-story Canada Lake House was a vision of William Claflin as the area's first planned resort. The Auskerada was sold to new owners, James M. Strong and Fred A. Cook, in 1916. (Courtesy of Barbara Donnelly.)

Travelers to the Auskerada registered from nearby communities, such as Johnstown and Fort Plain, as well as from towns requiring travel, such as Albany and Buffalo. The hotel had 100 rooms, a boathouse, shooting gallery, and billiard room. Room rates were $10.50 to $14 per week. A post office was located on the hotel's second floor. Mail was addressed to Auskerada, New York. (Courtesy of the Town of Caroga.)

The rhythm of life at the lakes is dependent on the freeze and thaw of the lakes themselves. Records are kept for most of the area lakes to show the dates of freezing and thawing (or "ice out"). Records show that in some years, ice arrived as early as October and did not leave the lakes until May, which meant that some camp owners, who traveled to camp by boat, could not access their properties until that time. Ice on the lakes was welcomed, however. It provided a new source of recreation, in the form of ice fishing and ice-skating. Thick slabs of ice served as "ice roads" from one side of the lake to the other. Blocks of ice were harvested for both residential and commercial use. In icehouses throughout the region, blocks would be stored until needed during the warmer months. (Courtesy of Richard and Judy Arthur.)

NEW YORK STATE TECHNOLOGICAL SURVEY OF CANADA LAKE

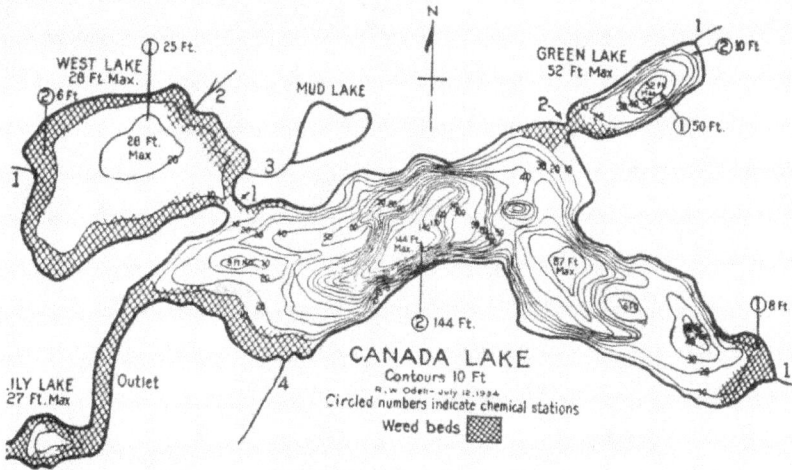

Chart 14. Canada, West and Green lakes

This 1934 New York State Technological Survey of Canada Lake shows the lakes' unique features. Canada Lake reaches a depth of 144 feet. In July 1924, Amy Menge, at age 17, swam around the perimeter of Canada Lake in 8 hours, 20 minutes. After losing 15 pounds to the water, she then danced in celebration until midnight at Nate Hawley's Dance Hall on Canada Lake. (Courtesy of David and Catherine Graves.)

Rufus Alex Greider (1817–1900), an artist who visited Canada Lake in 1896 to capture its natural history, wrote the following of the pollution brought by the local tanning and logging industries: "The bottom of the lake became coated with a brownish deposit, which destroyed the food upon which the young fish live, also the sawdust entered the gills and interfered with their breathing and killed them." (Courtesy of Richard and Judy Arthur.)

The Fulton House was built in 1888 by James Y. Fulton. On October 12, 1914, the *Morning Herald* reported, "Fire had broken out in the Fulton Hotel and the main part of the building was burning briskly. There was but little chance of saving any part of the structure. All guests were out of the hotel and safe at Vrooman's in Caroga Lake." (Courtesy of David and Catherine Graves.)

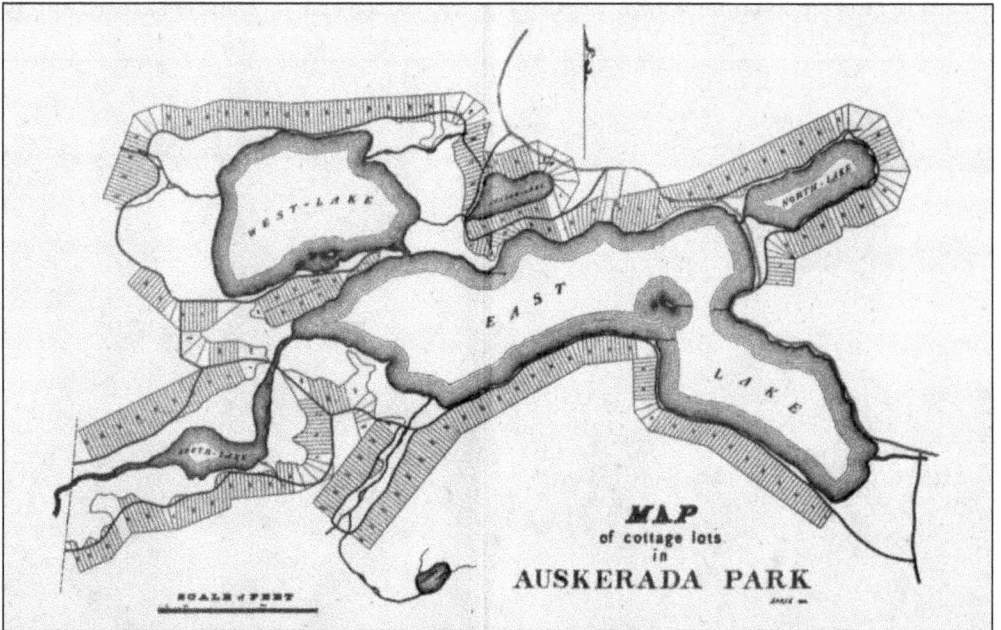

Alfred Dolge, an entrepreneur from nearby Dolgeville, envisioned a cluster of cottages around Canada Lake when he formed the Auskerada Park Club in 1897. Dodge, in his marketing attempt to attract only the finest (500) investors of "the most exclusive character," created a Native American chief, Aughstagradi, "the chief who catches many fishes," who lived at Auskerada Lake, "the-waters-of-many-fishes." In 1898, Dolge filed for bankruptcy. (Courtesy of Robert and Patricia Hagen.)

This is a photograph taken from Cave Rock, from where both Canada Lake and Stoner Island can be viewed. Around the mid-1930s, Elliot Roosevelt, who was visiting the area with his mother, Eleanor Roosevelt, lost his gold watch near the island when his fishing rig was hit unexpectedly by a bass fish. Although a trooper assigned to guard the family on this fishing expedition dove in after the watch, it was never recovered. Interesting treasures have been found during diving expeditions of the area's lakes, however. On August 1, 1999, while exploring Caroga Lake, 17-year-old scuba diver Matt Allen found a note in an old green champagne bottle. The note dated December 6, 1914, said, "Margaret 1:00. Cooking bull's head on the fireplace. The simple *leife* (life)." According to local legend, Nick Stoner, in an attempt to escape from Native Americans in pursuit, swam from the shore of Canada Lake to the island now bearing his name underwater. He used a hollow reed to get air. (Courtesy of Barbara Donnelly.)

Canada Lake's hermit, Jeff Reed, was known for his trout-catching skills, "Hill Billy Jam," outlandish costumes, beaver tail decorations on the exterior of his shanty, professional camp-care abilities, and "gone with the wind" notes he left on the door to his cabin. (Rumor has it that he may have played a mean shovel, too.) Reed was a storyteller who liked to scare youngsters away from his favorite fishing holes with tales about toe-biting hippos. Some believed that Reed was in hiding from the mob. Although no one is quite certain from where he came, Reed died at Canada Lake in 1974, leaving $30,000 and only one known relative, a niece in Texas. (Courtesy of the Town of Caroga.)

Four

PINE LAKE

Pine Lake played a critical role in the growth of the area. The Wheeler-Claflin Company owned and managed a lumber mill here. Once bark was removed for tanning, the remaining logs were harvested. Today, fallen hemlock deep in the woods that never made it to the mill can still be found. It was a favorite spot for families to gather. The official mailing address for the area was Pine Lake until 1912. (Courtesy of the Town of Caroga.)

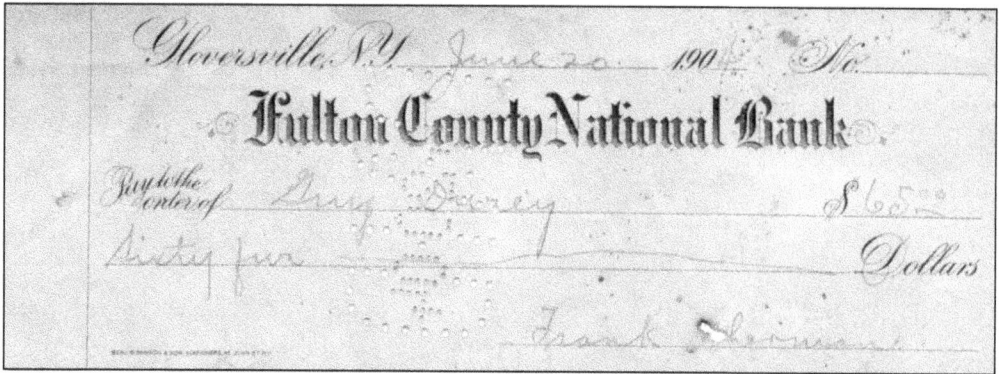

This check, dated June 20, 1904, and signed by Frank Sherman, was found in the attic of 'Neath the Pines, a summer camp owned by Raymond and Jean Parnell. Although the camp was used at one time as a dining room for lumberman, it is believed that Frank Sherman may have lived in this house during the time he operated a sawmill at Pine Lake. (Courtesy of Raymond and Jean Parnell.)

One man's misfortune can become another man's fortune. Such was the case at Pine Lake. Upon the 1924 bankruptcy of Frank Sherman, who had owned the land surrounding Pine Lake, Joseph Groshans (shown) purchased the land that would become Groshans' Park. One of his favorite rides was the 1903 C.W. Parker Carousel. Ride tickets for the carousel cost 12¢. The carousel sold at an auction in 1990 for about $204,150. (Courtesy of the Town of Caroga.)

Shown here in the mid-1920s is the Pine Lake swim area, with Roundtop Mountain in the background. On the back of the postcard, the sender wrote, "Children got undressed in bathhouse, 25¢ to go swim in this lake, dove off raft, very nice white sand." Although sand is found naturally in the area, most of the Pine Lake sand was carted in and spread by hand. (Courtesy of William and Chardel Houck.)

Sitting near the dam, Timberline Inn was built in the late 1800s. It was first used as a lumbering camp. For several years, it had the only phone at Pine Lake. Today, it is owned by Charles and Lois Svehla, who use it as a year-round residence. Some Pine Lake residents believe that a former spirit may still walk the house, turning on lights when no human is present. (Courtesy of Richard and Mary Groshans.)

Joseph Groshans opened his dance hall at Groshans' Park on Decoration Day, known today as Memorial Day, in 1925. Crowds gathered to listen to country bands and engage in energetic square dances. During its 80-plus-year history, the structure has weathered many storms, both financially and physically. Today, known as the Adirondack Paradise, summer residents and guests gather for weekly dances and specialty beverages, such as the "Speedo," named for a regular beachgoer. (Courtesy of Richard and Mary Groshans.)

Near the entrance to Pine Lake Park stands a home that is rich in history. Currently owned by the Hillock family and used as a year-round residence, this building was once the Pine Lake School, the Ram Pam Club, and a logging camp. Take note of the hanging pennant. Not only did locals collect school pennants, but many also collected lake pennants, including one for Pine Lake. (Courtesy of Margaret Western.)

Some Pine Lake campers purchased recycled building materials, originally used to construct temporary shelter for wounded soldiers at nearby Rhodes Hospital in Utica, to build their summer camps. In 1956, the William and Dorothy Schram family reassembled their cottage with the help of fellow campers. Construction started on July 7, and three weeks later, the family moved in. Shown at right is a record of the campers who assisted on this particular building project. Take note of the first signature on the page; it is that of Joseph Groshans, the owner of Groshans' Park and a friend of the campers. Today, the children and grandchildren of these original camp owners return to Pine Lake each summer to carry on the traditions of the lake. (Both, courtesy of Wayne and Nancy Seeley.)

This Camp was built through the kindness and generosity of our fellow campers.

It was started July 7, 1956 and we moved in three weeks later. Open house was held on Sunday, September 2, 1956.

This photograph from 1960 shows, from left to right, Christian Groshans, Richard Groshans, and Anna Groshans. Christian was brother to park owner Joseph Groshans. Christian assisted Joseph with the business. For 40 years, Joseph worked for the power company, walking a lake route that started at East Caroga Lake and ended at Pleasant Lake. Joseph also had a role in locally filmed *Ten Nights in a Bar Room*. He would die in 1961 without a will. (Courtesy of Richard and Mary Groshans.)

In the 1960s, the North-South Skirmish Association (N-SSA) gathered at Pine Lake. The N-SSA promotes the shooting of Civil War firearms and artillery and encourages the preservation and display of Civil War materials. As part of its mission, the N-SSA conducts live firings of Civil War firearms and artillery. At Pine Lake, cannon balls were fired into the lake. Today, some of these cannon balls still remain at the bottom. (Courtesy of family of Larry Holmes.)

Donna Rush is pictured here with singer Lynn Anderson, who performed at the Adirondack Paradise at Pine Lake in 1984 as part of the "Adirondack Nashville Show Schedule." Rush purchased the former Adirondack Pavilion and Amusement Park the same year. Other performers who took the stage beneath the pines under Rush's watch included The Kendalls, Shelly West, Box Car Willie, Louise Mandrell, and Tammy Wynette. (Courtesy of Wayne and Nancy Seeley.)

Lake history is filled with stories of young couples rowing across the water into the sunset, falling in love, eloping, and getting married. Pine Lake has become a wedding destination point, with couples saying "I do" on the beach. On August 7, 2010, Michelle Congdon and Robert Servidone tied the knot. The first recorded wedding in the town of Caroga was of Francis Vandercook and Lucy Jeffers in 1800. (Courtesy of Jeffrey Houck.)

Pine Lake was almost lost in 2006, when devastating floods weakened the earthen dam. New York State Department of Environmental Conservation (DEC) insisted that the dam be replaced. Unfortunately, the dam fell on privately owned land, and the landowners bore the expense to replace the dam, one that would benefit all lake property owners and campground guests. This was not the first flood to threaten the lake. In April 1966, when the park was owned by Robert Lord, heavy rains washed out a section of the dam. Workers scrambled to reinforce the structure. Earlier, in 1913, water broke through the dam completely. The photograph below shows a construction worker imprisoned within the rebar of the new dam prior to pouring the concrete. (Both, courtesy of Raymond and Jean Parnell.)

Five

OTHER LAKES AND AREAS

Harwood Rowles models with his summer trout catch in 1901. The fish were taken from Bellows Lake, located northeast of Canada Lake. Bellows Lake was one of several local lakes that were stocked with trout by New York State. One summer, in an attempt to stock the lake from a low-flying aircraft, the pilot missed the lake completely, stocking nearby treetops with a ton of fish. (Courtesy of the Town of Caroga.)

Natural sweetener is harvested from the lake region. This photograph from the spring of 1924 shows a team of horses unloading sugar maple sap at a sugarhouse in the Stewart's Landing area. The sap was boiled down to make maple syrup, an Adirondack sweet treat. Forty gallons of sap are needed to make one gallon of syrup. (Courtesy of Wayne and Nancy Seeley.)

Although soil in the lake area was not suitable for farming, it was adequate for raising livestock. In the North Bush area, sheep were held in a common area and cared for. To identify each owner's livestock, ears were "marked." The following was taken from local earmark record books: "1793. Recorded June 22. John Matthews Mark of Cattle and Hoggs. A Square Crop in the Left Ear, and a Slit in the Right Ear." (Courtesy of the Town of Caroga.)

As seen in 1910, Camp Ruffit on Green Lake was part of a tent colony from 1909 to 1918. This photograph was taken by one of the several professional Adirondack postcard photographers who traveled the area to stage scenes and capture memories. Today, these postcards are traded and collected. Note that there is no netting on this tent opening to prevent black flies and mosquitoes from sharing the space. (Courtesy of the Town of Caroga.)

A wooden bridge marks the junction of Green Lake and Canada Lake in the early 1900s. Martin and Elizabeth Kennedy Sr. take a rowing excursion with their grandchildren, Rachel Briggs and Everett Briggs. In 1981, the Canada Lake Protective Association added 26 tons of lime to Green Lake in an attempt to make the lake less acidic. Like many lakes in the Adirondacks, Green Lake became acidic, perhaps from acid rain. (Courtesy of the Town of Caroga.)

In the late 1800s, a sawmill, owned by James Stewart, operated in what became Stewart's Landing. Many of the workers came from Irish Settlement, a small community near the town of Stratford. The dam at Stewart's Landing was critical, not only for the operation of the sawmill, but also to help maintain the level of Canada Lake and its sister lakes, Green Lake, Lily Lake, and West Lake. The dam also allowed for steamer travel. Those coming from Dolgeville and areas west of the lakes could travel by steamer up to camps and hotels. Those staying at the hotels could take a leisurely tour of the lakes, which included a ride down to Stewart's Landing, by steamer. The three-hour round-trip cost about 50¢. (Above, courtesy of Margaret Reaney Memorial Library; below, courtesy of the Town of Caroga.)

The latest dam at Stewart's Landing was built in 1922 by Adirondack Power and Light. A pipeline extended from the base of the dam for the Sprite Creek Hydro Electric Plant to a surge tower, which could be seen from miles away. During the construction of the tower, one of the construction crew members fell 180 feet to his death. Once completed and in operation, leaks would occasionally spring along the pipeline. During warm-weather months, local residents would gather around the leaks with a bar of soap and take showers. Today, camps line the water above the dam, and the state controls the level of water at the dam. (Both, courtesy of Wayne and Nancy Seeley.)

This group, including artist Clare Dwiggins (second row, far right), gathers in front of the dam at Irving Pond. The first Irving Pond dam was built in 1855 to power a sawmill owned by James Irving. A replacement dam was constructed by Niagara Mohawk Power Corporation in 1926. In 1997, that dam was demolished due to structural concerns. Today, with no dam, local residents voice concerns over potential flooding downstream at Canada Lake. (Courtesy of Dona Dise.)

Before Wheeler-Claflin arrived in the area, there were a few small tanners in the area. One was Platt Potter, who tanned in the early 1860s. About the same time, Thomas J. Potter operated a sawmill. Shown here is Potters Pond Dam at Wheelerville in 1923. Historians are uncertain as to which operation this dam was associated with. (Courtesy of the Town of Caroga.)

Shown here in 1915 with his sled dog is Tony Beekman, who was also known as Mr. Green Lake. Beekman enjoyed his camp and the many antics that happened there on the northern lake extension to Canada Lake. Beekman kicked up a little mischief in 1906 when he rode the first motorcycle through the lake area. (Courtesy of the Town of Caroga.)

The first residents of the Stoner Lakes area were Native Americans. Stoner Lakes were the last of the lakes in the area to be settled. Nick Stoner called them Stink Lakes because of the smell released by dead fish found on the downside of a beaver dam. They were also known as Beaver Lakes and Vrooman Lake and DeLine Lake. Today, they are East and West Stoner Lakes. (Courtesy of the Town of Caroga.)

Several lakes throughout the Adirondacks are called Pleasant Lake. Shown here, lying just west of Pine Lake and Nine Corner Lake, is North (Big) Island at Pleasant Lake. Although small in size, Fulton County is home to 44 lakes, which has made the area marketable not only for tourism and recreation but also for industry, as water has been needed in the past to operate sawmills and tanneries and provide ice. (Courtesy of Robert Fear.)

A favorite pastime at the area's lakes is fishing. Here, in 1959, is Edith Korrow, as she uses a long pole to fish for dinner in West Stoner Lake. The following is from an August 1893 edition of the *Fulton County Republican*: "[Fishing] is not as 'it onct was.' There was a time when [fish] were so numerous that swimming in the lake was actually impossible." (Courtesy of Jeannine Schwartz.)

Six

BUSINESS, INDUSTRY, AND TOURISM

To survive in the Adirondack Mountains in the 19th century, one had to be resourceful. Eune Arnst , an immigrant from Switzerland, settled on London Bridge Road in 1869, working as a cobbler, shingle maker, and barber. Arnst also served as "overseer of highways" in the mid-1880s. Today, his cobbler tools and shed are located on the grounds of the Caroga Museum. (Courtesy of the Town of Caroga.)

WHEELERVILLE

Scale 30 Rods to the Inch.

Bark &
Leach House
Boiler
Beam House
Dry & Finishing House
Office
Barn
L.Wheeler
Wheeler & Claflin
School
J.Richards

S.M.
S.M.
Store
B.S.Sh.

Business Directory
J.M.Wheeler, Tanning & Lumb
M.Barns, Saw Mill & Lumber
Dealer
L.Wheeler, Tanner
P.Potter, Tanner

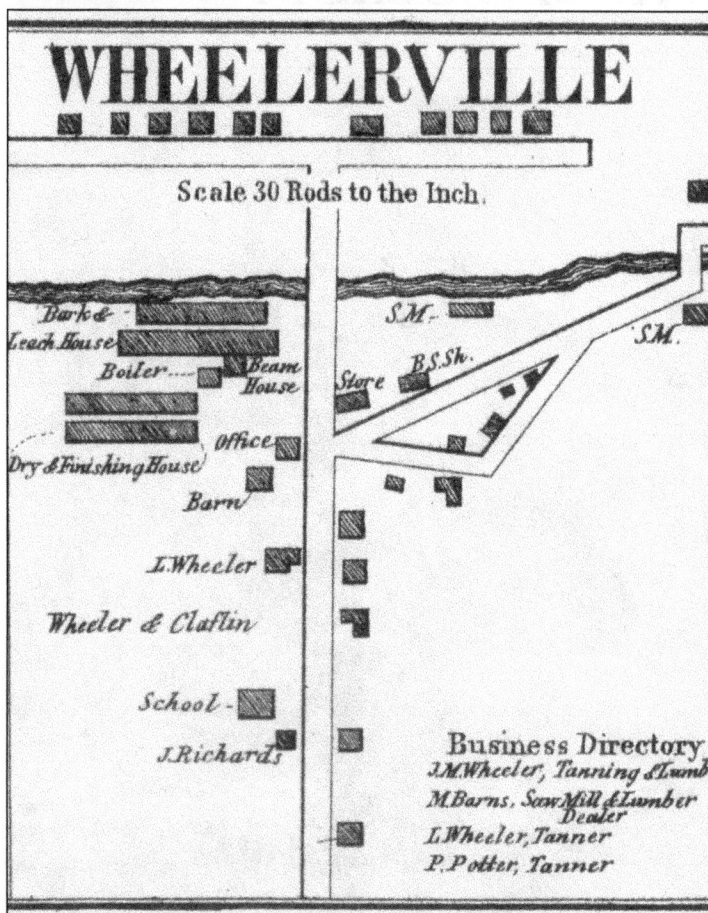

The tannery at Wheelerville changed the landscape of the community. William Claflin purchased 20,000 acres of hemlock-rich land in 1865. Claflin needed hemlocks for the tannin and water for his steaming operation. The tannery site included a vat and leaching sheds, two drying sheds, and a barn. The tannery sheds housed vats that consumed 7,000 cords of hemlock bark in which about 25,000 skins were processed, producing 250 tons of leather. The Wheeler-Claflin Company employed about 14 people in the tannery, with almost 100 workers in the woods. Today, the barn is the Nick Stoner Inn. (Both, courtesy of the Town of Caroga.)

Dry Goods

		1504	61
1 Doz Playing cards		2	00
Arnica Plaster			25
2 Pair Boys slippers	25	.	50
7 clocks	1.75	12	25
1	—	1	00
3	—	3	00
8 Boxes Dominoes	1.00		67
1½ Doz. Pipes	1.00	1	50
1 Box shav. soap			90
2 Neck Ties	25	.	50
1 Roll Oilcloth curtain 14		6	72
2 " Table oilcloth	2.00	4	00
3 — shelf " "	65	1	95
2 Balls	50	1	00
6 Rolls Pa curtain	25	1	50
6 Mouthorgans	50	3	00
3 Pr stockings	8		24
10 " Boys stocking	7		70
		1546	29

This 1884 ledger from the Wheelerville Tannery Company Store shows part of its dry goods inventory. The total inventory for the store at the time was $5,903.32. Take note of the following items listed as inventory: a dozen decks of playing cards totaling $2, neckties valued at 25¢ each, 11 clocks, 6 mouth organs at 50¢ each, and 18 pipes at $1 a dozen. Other items not shown on this page but worth noting are 114 pounds of "Jap Tea" at 30¢ a pound, 11 spittoons at 14¢ each, 3 looking glasses at $1 a piece, and kerosene at 30¢ a gallon. Most of this inventory arrived by horse-drawn carriage or steamer. The store closed in 1893. (Courtesy of Caroga Historical Association and Museum.)

The Durey Land and Lumber Company, operated by Guy and Cyrus Durey, was formed for two things, land and lumber. After clearing land for its lumber, lots were sold for camps. The Durey Company was the largest operating sawmill in Fulton County. It burned down in 1926, unbeknownst to the fire observer, James C. Luff, at Kane Mountain, who had not realized it had succumbed to fire until the next day. At the time, it was being leased by Julius Breckwoldt of Dolgeville. The photograph below shows the Durey operation in 1905. Durey would enlarge the operation in 1912. During World War I, the mill employed over 100 men. Cyrus Durey, this mill, and the need for water for its operation were all instrumental in the development of the new dam at Stewart's Landing. (Both, courtesy of the Town of Caroga.)

Jack Durey sits atop a pile of logs at the Pine Lake or Wheeler-Claflin Mill. The first sawmill at Pine Lake was built around 1870. The 106-by-65-foot mill contained 29 saws and was built to use what remained of the logs in nearby Wheelerville's tanning process. In the photograph below, finished wood products are stacked at Pine Lake. The plank road, known as a corduroy road due to its appearance, was extended at a cost of about $7 per rod from Wheelerville to Pine Lake to help move lumber down to the railroad in Fonda, where it was transported to other areas. Milling at Pine Lake ended in 1911, when the sawmill, owned by Frank Sherman, burned. Sherman would file for bankruptcy. (Both, courtesy of the Town of Caroga.)

At the triangle between the Johnstown and Gloversville Roads in 1878, Joseph Sherman built the first hotel in the lake region. The Caroga Hotel was run by Joseph Sherman, a carpenter and politician, and his wife, Elizabeth. Their son Frank joined the business in 1894 and quickly learned the lake's hospitality and entertainment business. The Caroga Hotel was lost to fire in 1899, and Frank Sherman left the area. (Courtesy of Donald and Erma Hoffman.)

The Unger House, at Five Points, could board up to 20 people and feed up to 100 in its dining hall. One meal included the infamous Al Capone, who was on his way to Speculator, New York. On September 20, 1930, the Unger House was struck by lightning. The local paper reported that "nothing was saved from the hotel with the exception of a small amount of canned vegetables carried from the kitchen." (Courtesy of the Town of Caroga.)

Hotels at the lakes, including Sherman House at Caroga Lake, marketed themselves as a place for rest and physical recovery. The following letter, dated July 10, 1897, captures the healing spirit of the lake region well: "My Dear Friend Mr. Spooner, I suppose you have thought many times that I was not going to write to you . . . I am feeling much better. The air is dry and pure that is seems that I shall fill up nearly to my toes at every breath. I have a good board and plenty of it. I have been fishing some and enjoy it very much. I am getting a good color on my face and hands and arms. I take a five o'clock boat ride nearly every morning, then put up my hammock and lazy off till it cools off some then go out boating, shooting, or riding. The people here are very good to me. A.A. Dorn" (Courtesy of the Town of Caroga.)

In 1910, artist Clare Dwiggins sent this illustrated envelope to Cyrus Durey. In addition to being an influential businessperson, he was a politician. Durey held several local and national positions, including US representative from New York for the 60th and 61st congress. He was unsuccessful in his reelection campaign in 1910 for the 62nd congress. He was successful, however, in forming the town's history. It was Durey who memorialized Nick Stoner. After the dedication of the Nick Stoner Memorial, New York State Assembly member and Canada Lake resident Eberly Hutchinson wrote the following: "It is doubtful whether there would be any memorial of Caroga's ancestral hero other than Simms's pages and Stoner's tombstone, had it not been for the interest in local antiquity of Cyrus Durey, and his desire to add historic appeal to the natural charms of our region." Today, Nick Stoner is remembered not only through the Nick Stoner Memorial at the Nick Stoner Golf Course but also with Stoner Island at Canada Lake and East and West Stoner Lakes. (Courtesy of the Town of Caroga.)

In the late 1950s, lumberman Gregory Ashlaw harvested over a million board feet of birch and other hardwoods from the bottom of Canada Lake. The logs had originally been harvested by the Durey Land and Lumber Company, shown above, but while floating across the lake to the mill site, they sunk. Ashlaw affixed chains to the logs, brought the wood to the surface, and then floated the logs using barrels to shore. (Courtesy of David and Catherine Graves.)

In 1916 under new ownership, the Auskerada became the Allen Inn. Its new life was shortened on August 23, 1921, just one week before a planned opening, when, while removing old flooring in the bar room, "a fire of unknown original . . . destroyed the Allen Inn with a loss of about $25,000." (Courtesy of the Town of Caroga.)

Gene Groshans, William Morris, and Chris Groshans helped to harvest over 1,000 blocks of ice, each 19–21 inches a side, from Pine Lake during one winter season. The ice was needed to support Groshans' Park during the summer months. Alvarado Arnst remembered the ice harvests on Canada Lake, which required the use of horse and plow, as follows: "We filled icehouses for ten dollars. We stopped cutting when electricity came through, about 1930. Everybody got electric ice boxes, and we felt we were living on the top shelf." In the photograph below from the 1940s, Carmela Colangelo stands before the second Unger Icehouse. In 1977, space at the Unger Icehouse was donated to the Caroga Historical Association and Museum to house exhibits depicting life in the lake region, including ice harvesting. (Above, courtesy of Richard and Mary Groshans; below, courtesy of Jerry and Kim Groom.)

From 1925 to 1931, the Fulton County Fish and Game Club operated a State Fish Hatchery along Durey Creek in North Bush. Here, Gordon Spencer (left), hatchery caretaker, and John Wells/Walls (right) observe brown trout. Many of the lakes throughout the region were stocked by the state to promote tourism. The hatchery was relocated to Gloversville. (Courtesy of the Town of Caroga.)

The Caroga Hotel, on the right, caught fire one night during Prohibition. Men formed a bucket brigade to extinguish the fire. With each pail of water tossed onto the blaze, a case of beer was taken from the burning hotel and deposited in a "holding area" out of harm's way. With the fire out, the men gathered to celebrate, only to find their beer had been stolen. (Courtesy of the Town of Caroga.)

These cash registers were destined for Sherman's Park at Caroga Lake in 1922. Frank Sherman started the business one year earlier. Having watched Sherman experience financial misfortune once before when he filed for wood- and fire-related bankruptcy, Caroga Lake neighbors watched piles of lumber grow behind Sherman's house with curiosity. Rumor has it that this lumber was second quality lumber and could not be sold from his sawmill down on London Bridge Road. That lumber, however, was good enough to build a dance hall and bathhouse. From that time forward, all roads led to Sherman's Park at Caroga Lake, and Frank Sherman headed to the bank with his profits. These signs were posted on trees leading to Caroga Lake and Sherman's Park from all directions. (Above, courtesy of Donald and Erma Hoffman; below, courtesy of Joseph Ricciardi.)

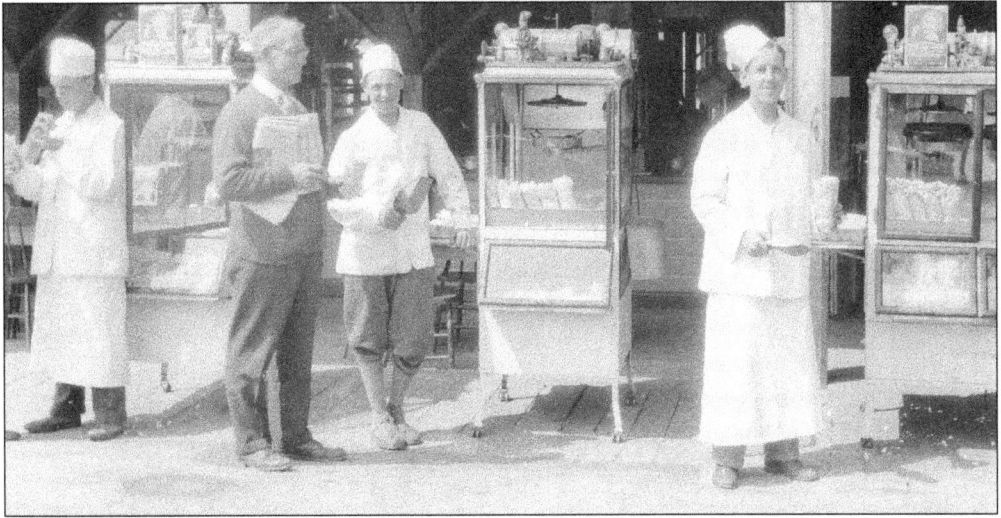

Visitors to Sherman's were welcomed by a lineup of popcorn connoisseurs. Shown in this photograph from the 1920s are, from left to right, Andrew Meyers, Frank Sherman Sr., Clarence Lewis, and Frank Sherman Jr. The two Sherman brothers, Frank Jr. and Floyd, would eventually take over the family business. Frank Sherman Sr. died in 1955 at the age of 86. (Courtesy of Donald and Erma Hoffman.)

Sherman's Park employed up to 50 people each summer. Seen in this photograph are, from left to right, (first row) Faye Allen, Helen Olyer, Vern Olyer, Erma Hoffman, and Harold King; (second row) Frank Sherman Jr., William Morris, Gordon Barney, Charles Landers, Charles Hobbs, unidentified, Martha Nixon, and Donald Hoffman. (Courtesy of Donald and Erma Hoffman.)

Not only was Sherman's a place for family fun, it was also a gathering spot for corporate picnics. Because of the close proximity of Caroga Lake to the cities of Johnstown and Gloversville, together known as the "Glove Cities," manufacturers of gloves and other products would often treat their employees and their families to days at Sherman's Park. Company picnics were not limited to leather-good companies, however. In 1961, employees from Remington Arms in nearby Ilion packed the pavement for a company picnic. Although Sherman's Park is now closed, corporations, such as Walmart, still head to the lakes to honor their employees and their families at Pine Lake. (Both, courtesy of Donald and Erma Hoffman.)

The bustling activity of Sherman's Park on June 19, 1948, required the assistance of three Fulton County Sheriff Department officers on site to park cars and maintain order. From left to right are Frances Arnst, Joseph Ricciardi Sr., and unidentified. Because the lake area is remote, there is no local police force. (Courtesy of Joseph Ricciardi.)

Once the Wheelerville Tannery foreman's home and a boardinghouse, the Christmas Tree Lodge was known for both shooting stars and its owners, Nora and Glenn Harris. Glenn Harris, a New York State assemblyman, proposed a bill in 1972 to place the dam at Stewart's Landing under state ownership. Route 10 is called the Glenn H. Harris Memorial Highway, and in 2010, a town park was erected to honor Harris. (Courtesy of David and Catherine Graves.)

Hollywood came to the area several times. In the 1920s photograph above, Blazed Trail Productions filmed a western movie along the banks of Canada Lake. For this Native American scene, actors were painted with grape juice to darken their skin. Fred Keating was one actor who spent time at the lakes working on Blazed Trail Production movies. In 1936, *The Last of the Mohicans* was filmed at Broomstick Lake, north of Pine Lake. In 1981, *Out of the Rain* was shot in the lake area and surrounding cities. Locals were often used to construct sets and serve as extras. Dr. John Larrabee reported digging up abandoned movie reels in his garden on his Canada Lake property. The photograph below shows an impromptu musical performance in 1917 with Blazed Trail Production company members and local residents. (Both, courtesy of the Town of Caroga.)

The State of New York constructed fire towers throughout the state's forest lands in an effort to protect its greatest resource. The 62-foot Kane Mountain steel tower was constructed in 1925 and abandoned by the state in 1988. Everett "Buckshot" Smith served as tower observer for six separate terms. In 2000, the Canada Lakes Protective Association adopted the tower. Shown below, a fire in 1877 devastated the Pine Lake side of Kane Mountain. Kane Mountain was home to two toboggan runs. The first ran down the south side of Green Mountain into Green Lake, but the southern sun caused it to melt too quickly. The second, built on the north side of Kane Mountain, brought sledders 800 feet down to and across Pine Lake. Blocks of ice were carried up the mountain to form the slide. Kane Mountain Fire Tower was listed on the National Register of Historic Places in 2001. (Right, courtesy of David and Catherine Graves; below, courtesy of Barbara Spraker.)

The area's post offices changed locations often. Here, the post office was housed at the store owned by James Whittacker, who served as postmaster in the 1920s. The store and post office were located across the street from the hotel called Vrooman's. At one time, there were post offices throughout the area at Pine Lake, Canada Lake, Green Lake, and Newkirks Mills. Today, there is one post office for the multiple-lake area. (Courtesy of Barbara Donnelly.)

The Stoner Lake Diner is seen here in 1926. Although Stoner Lake lies in a remote area, it is en route to Arietta and Piseco. In 1841, the New York State Legislature proposed that a road be constructed that extended from Newkirks Mills to Piseco, by way of Stoner Lake. At one time, the original mills were located where the outlet for Pine Lake met the outlet for Stoner Lake. (Courtesy of the Town of Caroga.)

The Pine Lake Store sat near the old hunting lodge, which later became the Timberline Inn and Pine Lake Lodge. Bringing fresh goods to local residents was not easy. Store proprietors would take frequent trips by horse and carriage down into the cities of Johnstown or Gloversville to obtain fresh meat, fruits, vegetables, and breads. (Courtesy of the Town of Caroga.)

Berghoff's Country Store brought the first gas pumps to the area. Gas, or perhaps the lack of gas, put the Caroga Lake area in the *New York Times*. During the oil embargo of 1973–1974, Clayton Shutts's gas station, which was the only one in town, ran out of gas. Residents could not get to work and lumbering in the area ceased. (Courtesy of the Town of Caroga.)

Hotel and theater magnates J. Myer Schine and Hildegard Schine built a summer home, "Myhil," near Caroga Lake. The home is seen here engraved on a silver 25th anniversary plate. Known visitors included Elvis Presley, Art Linkletter, Babe Didrikson, Gov. Thomas Dewey, and Senator McCarthy. Their son G. David Schine is known for his role in the 1954 McCarthy hearings. The Schines would invite guests to preview new films in their private movie studio. (Courtesy of Glove Theatre and Museum.)

Burt Kennedy is shown with Tyson Scott, a world champion trotter at 1 1/16 mile races. Tyson Scott was owned by Thunderbird Stables, located on Morey Road. Saratoga Springs, with the oldest horseracing track in the country, premiered *The Last of the Mohicans* on August 13, 1936. Some of today's races at Saratoga include names from the movie filmed at Broomstick Lake—Mohican Handicap, the Chingachgook Handicap, and the Magua Handicap. (Courtesy of the Town of Caroga.)

Seven

ARTS, CULTURE, AND EDUCATION

Artist Paul Bransom, a Canada Lake summer resident, created this picture of Durey's sawmill in 1920. Bransom is perhaps best known for his nature and wildlife work, however, he also illustrated Jack London's *Call of the Wild* and Kenneth Grahame's *The Wind in the Willows*, in addition to about 50 other books and hundreds of magazine articles. Upon his death in 1979, Bransom's ashes were scattered over Canada Lake. (Courtesy of the Town of Caroga.)

Canada Lake was a magnet for creative souls. Gathered together in 1918 are, from left to right, (standing beside porch) John Russell and unidentified; (sitting on the stairs) James Stanley (lying on rail), Maud Scriven, Lu Russell, Nell Stanley (sitting on rail), Grace Branson, Evangeline Russell, Paul Bransom, Teddy ?, and Jack Russell; (standing or sitting on the porch) Betsy Dwiggins, Clare Dwiggins, Phoebe Dwiggins, unidentified, Verne Scriven, Reg Scriven, Helen ?, two unidentified people, and Fred Keating. (Courtesy of Dona Dise.)

Clare Victor Dwiggins, known as Dwig, shares his cartoon-style artwork with his grandson Don. Dwig and his wife, Betsy Lindsay, discovered the beauty of Canada Lake in 1905 and purchased land and built a summer residence in 1907, where the artist was not only struck by inspiration but came close to being struck by lightning as he worked in his studio in 1935. Dwig was working at his art table when he felt the "need" to get up from the table and walk across the room. Seconds later, lightning struck the table. (Courtesy of Dona Dise.)

Clare "Dwig" Dwiggins first called his summer camp Mandalay. Later, it would be the Dwigwam. His art studio, where he created his daily panels and Sunday full-page cartoons, was located in a separate building on the property. Clare and pianist wife, Betsey Lindsay, would raise two children, Don and Phoebe, in this "ice out" home. Phoebe was born at Dwigwam. In Phoebe Dwiggins Ballard's biographical sketch of life at Canada Lake, she recalls one Fourth of July celebration when fireworks, while being transported out onto the water in a raft, ignited unexpectedly. The three boys on the raft dove into the water and guests at the celebration watched the flashlight trail of one of the boys as he swam for safety. Even Dwigs "did a wild war dance dodging and stamping out little flames that started up on the dry ground." Today, fireworks are launched from Stoner Island each Fourth of July. The Canada Lake Protection Association adopted Dwig's artwork in 1955 for its masthead, when it created its first *Echo* publication. (Courtesy of Dona Dise.)

Charles Sarka (1879–1960) and his wife, Grace Sarka, built a cottage at Canada Lake in 1910. For 50 years, they summered in the Southern Adirondacks. Sarka painted the mountains and water around him. One of his favorite subjects was Nick Stoner Island. This painting shows Dolgeville Point, so named because most of the first residents on this point were from Dolgeville. It was originally called Spruce Point. (Courtesy of the Town of Caroga.)

The Caroga Historical Association and Museum continue to foster the arts at the lakes by offering a variety of arts classes and hosting gallery shows. Past shows have included work by Charles Sarka, Paul Bransom, Rufus Alex Grider, and George Washington Waters. A quilt exhibit spotlighting 89 quilts inspired the town to create two town quilts, both of which are on display at the museum. (Courtesy of Caroga Historical Association and Museum.)

The Ralph Wadders Orchestra, shown here in 1925, performed at Sherman's Park at Caroga Lake. Years earlier, a rowboat carrying a German band, while returning to Stewart's Landing behind a steamer, began to take on water. The band, feeling refreshed from evening beverages, bailed the incoming water with their brass instruments. A piece of a brass, possibly part of an instrument, has been recovered from Canada Lake. (Courtesy of Donald and Erma Hoffman.)

In 1964–1965, locally known musicians would entertain Pine Lake Amusement Park guests on Sunday afternoons from atop of the game building. Because of its nice selection of rides for young children, Pine Lake Park drew family crowds and, therefore, offered family friendly entertainment. One of the more popular acts was "Willie the Clown" and his magic show. (Courtesy of William and Chardel Houck.)

The Wheelerville Methodist Episcopal Church was erected in 1872 as an extension of the Methodist Episcopal Society to serve the growing population of tannery workers and their families. The Gothic-style frame building was 27 feet wide and 51 feet long. The society was organized in 1842 by Stephen Parks of Stump City, also known as Gloversville. (Courtesy of the Town of Caroga.)

St. Barbara's Church at Caroga Lake served the Catholic faith starting around 1920. According to Lewis G. Decker, former Fulton County historian, St. Barbara's Church was partially constructed from materials dismantled at the former St. Joseph's Catholic Church in Bleecker, which had been built in 1856. Today, the property is owned Mark "Buzz" Van Etter, who purchased it in 2009 as a private residence. (Courtesy of David and Catherine Graves.)

Although the Caroga Chapel is used only in the summer by lake residents and visiting clergymen, many gathered there in the winter of 1972 to witness its demise due to winter snow weight. A crack started and spread, splitting the building in two parts before collapsing. Started in 1923, the chapel, sitting between the two Caroga Lakes, celebrated its 85th anniversary in 2008. (Courtesy of the Town of Caroga.)

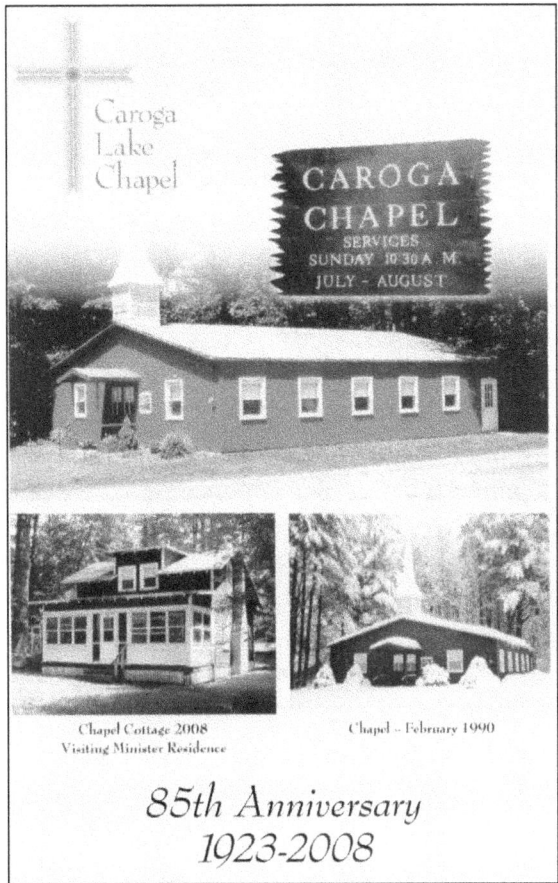

Caroga Lake Chapel

CAROGA CHAPEL
SERVICES
SUNDAY 10 30 A M.
JULY - AUGUST

Chapel Cottage 2008
Visiting Minister Residence

Chapel - February 1990

85th Anniversary
1923-2008

Amos King resided in North Bush before joining the 54th Massachusetts Regiment to fight in the Civil War. Pvt. Amos King was buried in the older section of the North Bush Methodist Church cemetery at the time of his death. On August 4, 1996, in a joint ceremony with the Peoples AME Zion Church of Gloversville, a grave marker was placed at his previously unmarked grave. (Courtesy of North Bush Methodist Church.)

81

The Wheelerville School was built in 1856 and, with several additions, operated at this site until 1991, when New York State Department of Education declared it inadequate. The new school was built near the East Caroga Lake outlet. At this location, a plaque was placed as a dedication to the late Staff Sgt. Harold P. Witzke III, who died in combat during Operation Desert Storm. On July 4, 1991, over 5,000 people attended a parade and fireworks celebration in his honor. The old school is now used for town business and as a medical facility. Perhaps one of the most unusual items ever listed on the town's budget was in the 1930s when $62.20 was appropriated for the purchase of food for resident deer that lived in a pen between the holes 7 and 9 on the town's golf course. (Above, courtesy of the Town of Caroga; left, courtesy of Joseph Ricciardi.)

Fern Dale School
District No. 4
North Bush, Town of Caroga,
Fulton Co., New York
1913—1914

BLANCHE A. STEINHOVER, Teacher

PUPILS

Martin Spencer
George Spencer
Stephen Spencer
Conrad Guenther
Ernst Guenther
Paul Guenther
Willard Durey
Alfred Durey
Beatrice Durey
Mary Spencer
Jennie Spencer
Evelyn Spencer

SCHOOL OFFICERS

Fred A. Stryker, Supt.
Lindridge J. Durey, Trustee
Richard Guenther, Clerk

Education is the apprenticeship of life

The Fern Dale School District No. 4 was nicknamed the "Durey School" for the following two reasons: Josiah Durey, who owned two sawmills along the Durey Creek, helped to build the school and many of the students in the school belonged to him or his extended family, including little Lena Durey, who attended the school as a fourth-grade student in 1899. Despite the grades shown in the image at right, Lena would graduate and become a schoolteacher. A school story that has been passed down through the generations involves one Julia Hickey, a teacher at the school around 1898. Hickey, who had a fear of goats, seemed to have many four-legged "encounters." A few students would be excused from school and assigned the task of "taking the goat home." Eventually, No. 4 closed in 1916, and students were reassigned to No. 3, the Shaw School. (Both, courtesy of the Town of Caroga.)

CARD OF STANDING

THIS IS TO CERTIFY,

THAT Lena Durey

a pupil of the 4 th grade in

District No. 4, Town of

Caroga
Fulton County, N. Y.

obtained the following standing in examination held Janv 26-7 1899 :

Spelling 48   Penmanship 90

Arithmetic 30   U. S. History —

Geography 80   Drawing 75

Language or
Grammar 95   Physiology 90

Reading 85   Civil Gov't —

Rosanna Smith Teacher.

WILLIS E. LEEK, Commissioner.

The Wheelerville Union Free School performs several plays each year. Here, in the 1940s, are, from left to right, (seated) Jean Whitman and Constance Sherman; (standing) Betty Rose Baker, William Moore, Margaret Smith, Richard Groshans, Eugene Groshans, and Nancy Bush. On May 11, 1959, about 80 students performed an original production, called *Legacy of the Lakes in Play and Pageant* by Canada Lake resident and elementary schoolteacher Marion "Bonnie" Buchner. The play was part of the Hudson-Champlain Year of History Celebration. The play introduced an audience of over 300 people to local Native American history, trapper Nick Stoner, life at Sherman's Park, talk during a quilting bee, and the origination of names of and around the lakes. (Above, courtesy of Richard and Mary Groshans; left, courtesy of the Town of Caroga.)

In 1937, Girl Scouts gathered at the entrance of the dining hall at Camp Kowaumkami, which was first attended in 1925 by Fulton County Scouts. The camp was located east of Caroga Lake, along a small stream that was dammed to create a pond for the scouts. Camp Kowaumkami later became the Mohawk Pathway Y Camp. No longer used as a camp in 1984, a group of volunteers disassembled the historic pegged barn and moved it to the present site of the Caroga Museum, where it now serves as a permanent exhibit hall, art gallery, and workshop area. The Girl Scout movement in the area was spearheaded by Martha Kunkel. (Above, courtesy of Caroga Historical Association and Museum; below, courtesy of Fulton County Museum.)

Wheelerville Union Free School sported a football team in 1946. Although the team was short on uniforms, it was tall on spirit when they defeated Fort Plain. Those pictured are, from left to right, (kneeling) Jerry Baker, Harold King, Robert Snell, Ronald Morris, and Clayton Shutts; (standing) George Holliday, Donald Baker, Robert Sweet, Eugene Smith, Bruce Busch, Frank Groshans, and Albert Snell. (Courtesy of George and Shirley Holliday.)

Fourth-grade students at Wheelerville Union Free School visit the Caroga Museum as part of their study of state history. Here, Kaaren Daniels explains the process of wool making to students. In the background is one of two Caroga quilts, with each quilt square depicting a facet of lake life. The quilt project was created by local seamstresses. In the 1990s, the quilts were displayed at a history conference in Utica, New York. (Courtesy of Caroga Historical Association and Museum.)

As part of the nation's bicentennial celebration in 1976, Boy Scout Troop 14 raised the bicentennial flag before the statue of Nick Stoner on the Stoner Golf Course. Like many communities around the country, the town of Caroga participated in numerous anniversary celebrations, including a large countywide parade in Gloversville. Local Boy Scouts camp in Bleecker at Camp Woodworth, which is part of the Twin Rivers Council. (Courtesy of the Town of Caroga.)

Assisted by Caroga Museum director Dorianne Gray, the Fulton County Arts Council held its Southern Adirondack Festival along the shores of West Caroga Lake on July 13, 2003. Hundreds gathered to hear Adirondack tall tales, listen to folk music, observe crafts being made, meet local authors, and attend workshops. As part of the celebration, Sherman's Park was open, and attendees could experience the old amusement park rides. (Courtesy of Caroga Historical Association and Museum.)

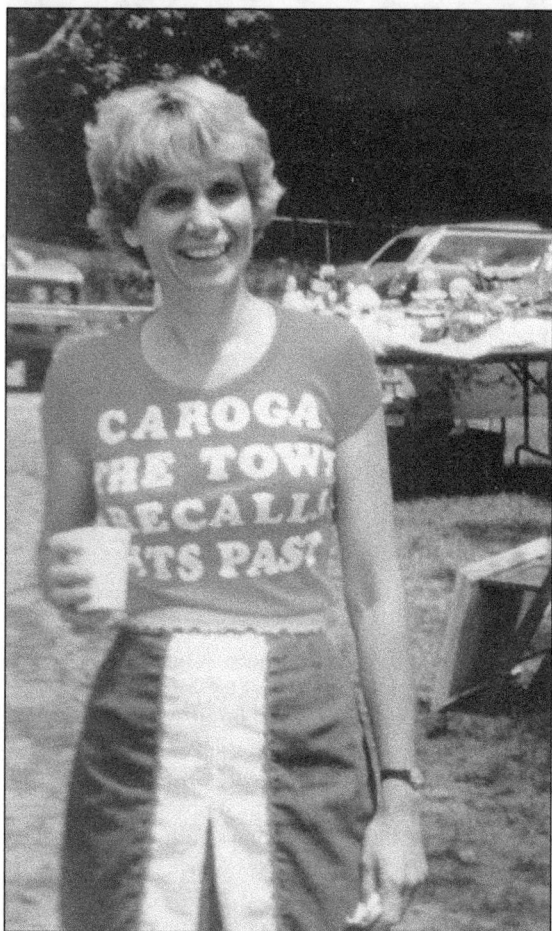

Before becoming the residence of Barbara McMartin and her husband, W. Alec Reid, the Lake View House on Canada Lake hosted both overnight guests and those who wished to enjoy a summer's treat of ice cream. McMartin (1931–2005) is the author of 25 books, including the *Discover* series of books about the Adirondacks. As part of the town's bicentennial celebration in 1976, McMartin interviewed residents and then wrote a book about the history of the town. A second edition, called *Caroga, an Adirondack Town Recalls its Past*, was released in 1998 and used as a resource for Images of America: *Around Caroga Lake, Canada Lake, and Pine Lake*. McMartin served on numerous state agency committees. In addition to sharing her passion for local and Adirondack history with readers and visitors, McMartin held three degrees in mathematics. Many considered Dr. McMartin to be the "tireless apostle of the Adirondacks." (Above, courtesy of David and Catherine Graves; left, courtesy of the Town of Caroga.)

The best-known musician in the lake area is the common loon. Adirondack folksinger Dan Berggren, while at a concert at Caroga Museum in 2004, sang about the musical waterfowl—"Like the voice of the loon, that carries its tune, north, east, south, and west. Over your land and my land, low land and high land, a song of the wilderness." The loon and its nests are protected throughout the area. (Courtesy of Darla J. Oathout.)

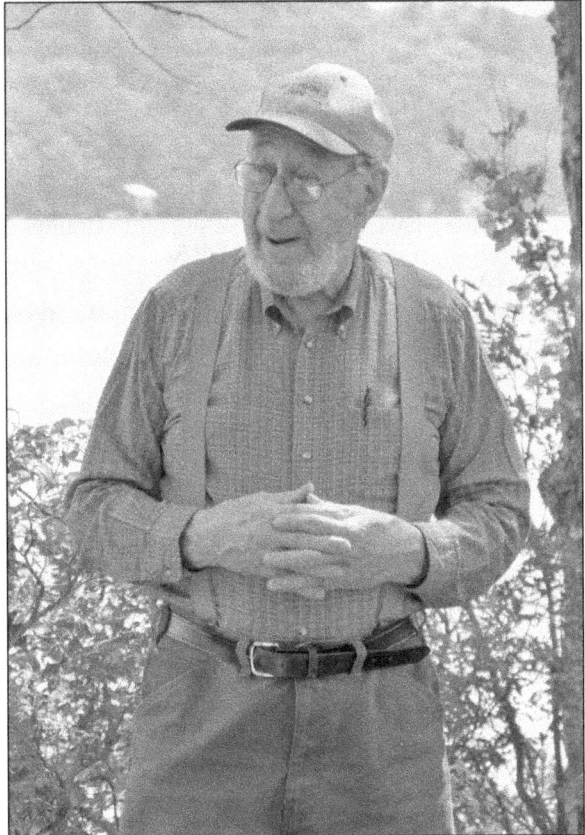

Adirondack storytellers, such as Don Williams, continue to bring history to audiences young and old. In this photograph, Williams stands upon Stoner Island weaving yarns of mountain days of past. Stoner Island is home to "Brown Bag Stories on the Island," and children arrive by boat to hear stories, read books, and enjoy a snack. Williams is the author of several books in Arcadia Publishing's Images of America series. (Courtesy of Linda Fake.)

For 90 years, Canada Lake resident Marion "Bonnie" Yates Buchner has tap danced throughout the country, winning numerous awards, while being recognized for her accomplishments by the National Dance Museum in Saratoga Springs, New York. Buchner continues to manage the Lakeside Motel and write. Throughout her life, Buchner has written many things, including speeches for former New York governor Nelson Rockefeller. In 2010, friends and family celebrated her 90th birthday and the 50th anniversary of the Lakeside Motel. Once called the Little Allen Inn, the motel claims to have the longest bar in Fulton County. Buchner turned down an opportunity to dance with the Radio City Music Hall Rockettes in the late 1930s. Instead, she went to Cortland State, where she studied to be a teacher. In 2006, she was inducted into the State University of New York at Cortland Hall of Fame, and in 2011, she appeared on Paula Abdul's *Live to Dance*. (Courtesy of Richard and Judy Arthur.)

Eight

RECREATION

Built along West Caroga Lake by Orville and Edward Vrooman, the first Vrooman hotel, known as the Lake View House, had a slide that extended out into the water. In addition to the slide, the hotel had a small amusement park, which was the first for the area, and it housed the Pine Lake Post Office. The hotel burned in 1904, under the ownership of George Fort. (Courtesy of the Town of Caroga.)

In 1907, Edward Vrooman turned a large farmhouse into another "Vrooman's hotel." A small amusement park stood behind it on West Caroga Lake. The amusement park was home to several pet bears, kiddie rides, a merry-go-round, and games of chance. The small park drew crowds from 1910 to 1920. A few years later, Children's Day was celebrated at Sherman's Park, shown here in 1922. Father to children of his own, Frank Sherman envisioned his park as a place for families to spend the day. On Children's Day, Caroga's youngest residents were treated to rides on ponies and in pony-pulled carts. (Courtesy of Donald and Erma Hoffman.)

In the 1920s, the beach at Sherman's Park on West Caroga Lake was reminiscent of Coney Island in New York City. Its white sand and diving tower drew summer crowds who would come to swim during the day and then dance at night. Here, in the background, is the Sherman's Park Complex, with its carousel building, dance hall, and bathhouses. (Courtesy of Robert Fear.)

Under the ownership of Joseph Groshans in the 1920s, the beach at Pine Lake drew large crowds of summer bathers and picnic goers. After the death of Groshans, Robert Lord purchased the park in 1961 as part of an estate settlement for $70,600. He changed the name from Groshans' Park to Pine Lake Amusement Park and added a campground to the complex. (Courtesy of William and Chardel Houck.)

From 1921 until the park was sold to the Morris family in 1970, the Sherman family offered a wide variety of amusement attractions at Sherman's Park. From swings that carried riders out over the water to ballroom dancing to the sounds of a variety of bands, there was something there for everyone. Seen above, under the cone-shaped canopy, and below, under a more permanent house, is the wooden carousel. It was crafted by German immigrant Charles Louff. It was first enjoyed in Sylvan Beach before being purchased by the Shermans and moved to Caroga Lake. Many of the concession stands on the midway were run by Thomas DeVine, whose son Thomas Jr. would later continue on their operation. (Above, courtesy of David and Catherine Graves; below, courtesy of the Town of Caroga.)

Pine Lake Park hailed itself in the 1960s as the largest amusement park for adults and children in Central New York. It had a roller coaster, whip, merry-go-round, bumper cars, orbit, and Ferris wheel. During this time period, the park was owned by Robert Lord, who created the hand-drawn map of the park below. Lord would operate the park until the 1970s, when it was sold off in parcels to different buyers. Today, most of the park is owned by the William Houck family, who operates the park complex under three different corporations. In 2011, the family will celebrate its 40th anniversary of ownership. William Houck and John Ivancic first became involved with the Pine Lake operations back in the 1960s when they operated the games area on the midway. (Above, courtesy of William and Chardel Houck; below, courtesy of the Town of Caroga.)

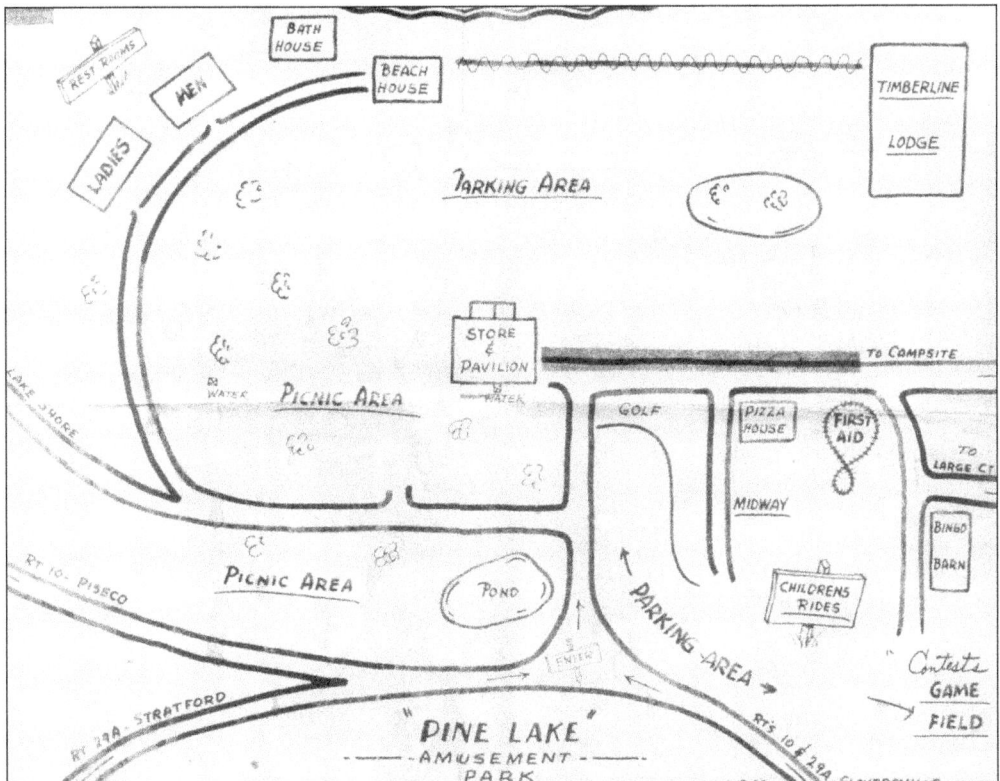

Dance halls were plentiful throughout the area, but perhaps the most popular was the hall at Sherman's Park, where Charles Mechino was dance master. He is pictured here in this 1920s photograph with an unidentified dance partner. On Sundays, buses would arrive from Albany and patrons could dance for the entire day to several orchestras. Dancers could purchase a ticket for a dime a ticket or three for a quarter. (Courtesy of Donald and Erma Hoffman.)

The arcade at Sherman's sported an array of games and activities. One of the more popular areas was the medallion-making machine, where guests could stamp their name onto a keepsake. The Caroga Museum, with a gift from Janet Sherman Shepard, daughter of Frank Sherman, created a building for an arcade and exhibit to capture childhood memories at the arcade and the inventive genius of her father. (Courtesy of Caroga Historical Association and Museum.)

The first unofficial downhill ski area was at Kane Mountain, where ambitious ski enthusiasts had to climb to the top of the mountain to ski down the wooded slope on the Pine Lake side. Although there was an effort in the 1930s to promote winter sports in the area, a lack of motorized equipment to get skiers back to the top of the run hampered marketing efforts. (Courtesy of Richard and Mary Groshans.)

Girls came from all around Fulton County to attend Girl Scout Camp near Caroga Lake. Here, they practice their diving skills at Camp Kowaukami. The pond was made specifically for the campers by damming a small creek that ran through the camp area, just east of Caroga Lake. Buses brought girls from villages around the county to participate in the scouting program. (Courtesy of Fulton County Museum.)

Once part of the Wheeler-Claflin Tannery that operated from 1865 to 1888, the Nick Stoner Golf Clubhouse served as the company store. The store's construction allowed farm wagons to pull up and into the building to load and unload under cover. In the early 1930s, the store was converted to the clubhouse. The course's first six holes were ready for play in 1925. Holes 7 and 8 were ready for play in 1926. The remainder of the course was ready in 1929, the date of this promotional piece for the Nicholas Stoner Club. As part of the Caroga Recreation Park, conceived by Cyrus Durey in 1922, the plans originally included an airfield and sightseeing trips of the lakes. The golf course was constructed on land originally owned by Durey Land and Lumber Company. (Both, courtesy of Caroga Historical Association and Museum.)

THE NICHOLAS STONER CLUB
OPEN TO THE PUBLIC
For the Season of 1929 — July 1st to December 1st
TOURISTS and VACATIONISTS ACCOMODATED
Large Comfortable Sleeping Rooms
European or American Plan
GOLF — TENNIS — FISHING — HUNTING — BATHING AND ALL OUT DOOR SPORTS
Beautifully Situated Between Caroga and Canada Lakes, Heart of the Adirondacks
60 Miles from Albany via Schenectady, Amsterdam, Johnstown and Gloversville
WHERE DEER ARE PLENTIFUL
Reservations made for Private Dinner and Dance Parties

CALL OR WRITE—The Nicholas Stoner Club, Phone 7060-F-2, Caroga Lake, N. Y.
GEORGE DUDLEY, Manager

Construction of the state-owned campground on East Caroga began in 1928. Due to the state's fiscal crisis in 2010, after 80 years of operation, the New York State Department of Environmental Conservation (DEC) announced the campground's closure. Friends of Caroga Lake Campground raised some funds to keep it open. The town, due to an unexpected inflow of revenue, also contributed to the campground's operating fund to keep the campground operating. Camping was, and continues to be, a popular activity at all of the lakes. The photograph below shows a typical camping scene in the 1950s at Pine Lake, where families would arrive late in the springtime and establish their campsite for the summer. (Above, courtesy of Arthur and Jane Bornt; below, courtesy of Wayne and Nancy Seeley.)

During the mid-1900s, horseback riding was offered at Green Lake. The old logging trails provided access to remote areas that could be reached easily on horseback. From Green Lake, riders could also ascend to the top of Kane Mountain, where a view of the lake area awaited them below. (Courtesy of David and Catherine Graves.)

In 1950, the American Motorcycle Association's Gypsy Tour came to Caroga Lake. Gypsy Tours, started in 1920, were held on a single weekend throughout the country. Rides frequently took participants to scenic areas to picnic and socialize. The rides were suspended briefly during World War II. Note the misspelling of Caroga (Coroga) on the pennant. (Courtesy of Joseph Ricciardi.)

In 1961, these Pine Lake campers wandered into the old bathhouse and traveled back through time when they discovered old bathing outfits, which had once been rented. From left to right are Bruce Grainer, Lance Lord, Robert Schram, Dorothy "Dot" Schram, Walter Schram, Lorraine Grainer, Harold Neilsen, Patricia Looman, and Ernest Marz. Although Lorraine Grainer wears a "Miss Pine Lake" sash in good fun here, there was an official Pine Lake Miss America Contest held in the early 1970s. (Courtesy of Wayne and Nancy Seeley.)

In the 1960s, William Houck, shown here inside the games building, operated several game attractions at Pine Lake Park, including the fishing pond, basketball hoops, and duck pond. With his wife, Chardel, and sons, Jeffrey and Joel, the Houck family expanded their interest in the park, eventually owning the campground, RV park, beach, and dance hall. (Courtesy of William and Chardel Houck.)

Royal Mountain Ski Area began in 1956 when Frederick Saunders and his wife, Eleanore Ireland, purchased Royal Hill from Howard Stock. That December, with the help of local ski enthusiasts, the ski resort opened with a rope tow, two trails, and a lodge. Following Saunders's death in 1971, Ireland sold the resort. Today, Royal Mountain is owned by James Blaze, who has expanded the ski area and introduced summer motorbike racing. In 1990, the American Motorcycle Association held its National Hillclimb Championships there. The longest ski season, without snowmaking equipment, happened in 1971. The slopes stayed open continuously through April 18. On May 9, 1966, however, an unusual spring snowstorm covered the hill with 10 inches of snow. After a hike up the mountain, Donald Curtis and William "Doc" Charles skied to the bottom. (Above, courtesy of Jeannine Schwartz; left, courtesy of Joseph Ricciardi.)

At 12 years old, Donald E. Curtis trained at Royal Mountain Ski Area. He would go on to be named the US Eastern Ski Association Champion in 1960. Note the bare ground below the jump. Under the ownership of James Blaise, snowmaking equipment was added, extending the season and making skiing conditions more consistent. Local high school teams train and compete at Royal Mountain Ski Area. (Courtesy of Donald and Gerd Curtis.)

Posing at the top of Queen's Run at Royal Mountain Ski Area is a group of ski enthusiasts. To get to the top of the ski run in 1957, skiers used a T-bar life, designed and engineered by a Swiss inventor ? Constram, who visited Royal Mountain as part of the design process. Another run at Royal Mountain, Knight Run was originally the town's Sugar Road. (Courtesy of Donald and Gerd Curtis.)

This northern pike was pulled from Pine Lake in the late 1930s by ? Van Bramer. Stories abound about the "fish of yesterday." During the 1800s, anglers regularly pulled in trout weighing two to three pounds. Alvarado Arnst reportedly snagged a trout that weighed at least seven pounds out of Canada Lake. Guesthouses and hotels would string the day's catch in cellars. (Courtesy of Richard and Mary Groshans.)

The Caroga Recreation Clubhouse Building originally served as the barn of the Wheeler-Claflin Tannery operation. In the mid-1920s, the renovation for this building was performed by the Town of Caroga. Eventually, it would become the property of Cyrus Durey amidst some unusual and complicated property exchanges. Today, it is the Nick Stoner Inn. (Courtesy of David and Catherine Graves.)

The New York State Department of Environmental Conservation (DEC) has maintained cross-country ski trails throughout the Adirondack Park. Many of these trails serve as hiking paths to remote lakes and mountain peaks in the summer. Shown here is Charles Svehla as he skis in the Pine Lake area following an ice and snowstorm. The earliest loggers and trappers in the area relied on snowshoes to distribute their weight over a larger surface area. This allowed the traveler to navigate on top of deep snowfalls. Today, winter explorers use both cross-country skis and snowshoes to trek back trails to frozen vistas. (Courtesy of Charles and Lois Svehla.)

There is shortage of neither water nor wind in the lake area. In the photograph above, two navigators transport their day's catch in a wooden sailboat, with two sails, across Canada Lake. Behind the sailboat is one of the steamers that operated on the lake in the late 1890s and early 1900s to transport travelers, goods, and lumber. Sailing continued to be a preferred transportation method and sport throughout the 20th century. The Canada Lake Protective Association offers sailing lessons and competitions for both novice and master sailors each summer. Below, young sailors team up with seasoned sailors to learn the basics of sailing near Stoner Island on Canada Lake. (Above, courtesy of the Town of Caroga; below, courtesy of Linda Fake.)

The 1956 ribbon and 1957 Ice Queen plaque were won by Caroga Lake resident Barbara Kowalski, who, as part of her icy rein, was required to sit on a block of ice as her throne. The ice carnival included ice and other winter sports events. Although the Ice Carnival is no longer held, residents still find sport in other winter events, such as outhouse races across the ice. (Courtesy of Barbara Donnelly.)

Pine Lake camper Nancy Schram started a recreation program for fellow campers in 1966. Here, the group prepares to ride to nearby Stoner Lake. Today, Schram and her husband, Wayne Seeley, return in the summer to Pine Lake with their youth group to experience summers in the southern Adirondacks. (Courtesy of Wayne and Nancy Seeley.)

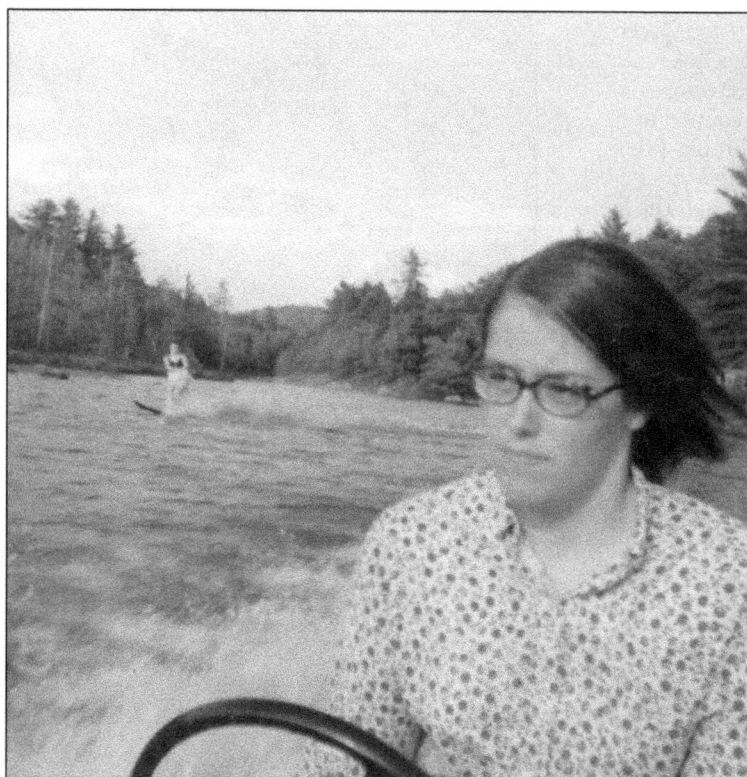

Jeannine White is pulled on water skis by sister Dianne White on West Stoner Lake in July 1968. Throughout the lake region, waterskiing is a popular sport. In 1999, the *Leader-Herald* newspaper spotlighted the skiing ability of 80-year-old Helen Mondato. To protect the habitat and lessen noise pollution, some lakes in the Adirondacks forbid the use of motorized equipment. (Courtesy of Jeannine Schwartz.)

The Caroga Fish and Game Club gathers here in the 1980s for its annual primitive rendezvous. Organized by Claude Burch in the late 1940s, the club is active in community programs, trout stocking, safety clinics, and shooting competitions. Each winter, the club hosts its ice fishing derby on Caroga Lake. The club is located on Hilley Road. (Courtesy of Caroga Fish and Game Club.)

At one time, the entrance to Pine Lake sported a pond filled with water lilies from around the world. From 1975 to 1984, however, that pond area was used for the popular lake sport of mud football. Over a 10-season stretch, local lake residents played teams from Fulton-Montgomery Community College (FMCC) in Johnstown. Brawn beat brain. Caroga won eight games. FMCC won one. The teams tied the remaining game. (Courtesy of Wayne and Nancy Seeley.)

Timothy and Samantha Rokos release their amphibious contestant in the frog jumping competition in 2004. The contest was part of a larger Southern Adirondack Festival, which brought storytellers, musicians, and artists to the shores of West Caroga Lake to celebrate mountain life, past and present. The brother-sister team took home the trophy that day, but not the frog. He was released into Caroga Lake. (Courtesy of Susan Rokos.)

Contestants were encouraged to kick up some sand during a sanctioned beach wrestling competition at Pine Lake in 2006 and 2007. The TNT Northeast National Beach Wrestling Championships offered matches for both male and female participants, including matches between the genders. Beach wrestling is performed standing inside a sand-filled circle measuring six meters (20 feet) in diameter. (Courtesy of Thomas Bergami.)

Pine Lake had its own sea serpent, shown here in the late 1970s. Local bars and restaurants competed in non-motorized boat competitions on the lake for cash prizes. In the past, local newspapers reported the possible sightings of a Loch Ness–type monster in the lake. To date, no proof has been found. (Courtesy of William and Chardel Houck.)

Watching wildlife is a popular activity. From the end of the Civil War until about 1980, moose sightings were rare throughout the Adirondacks. Moose volunteers in the three-lake area are currently collecting moose scat for DNA analysis. Scientists are trying to determine if moose in the area is due to migration or new births. This moose was photographed in 2010 north of Pine Lake. The State of New York Fisheries, Game, and Forest Law book is from 1899, which provides explicit instructions for fishing, hunting, and protecting state wildlife. The following is from the book: "No beaver should be caught or killed at any time in this state" and "A bounty of twenty dollars for each panther shall be paid." In 1968, two local residents reported the death of a 85-pound wolf found at Caroga Lake. Its identity was confirmed by state authorities. (Above, courtesy of Bart M. Carrig; right, courtesy of the Town of Caroga.)

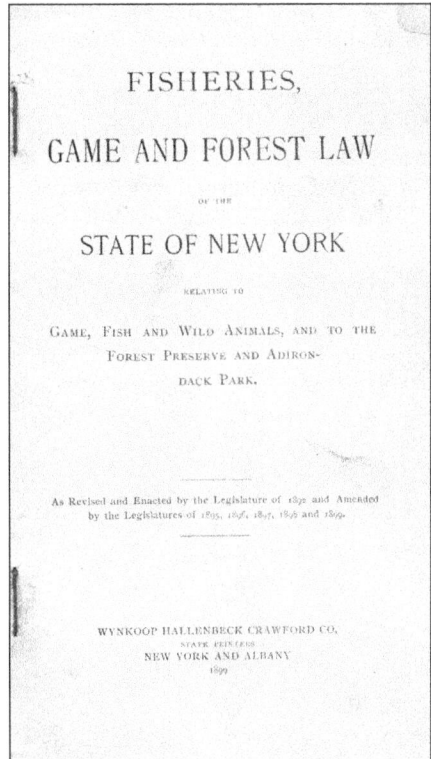

FISHERIES,

GAME AND FOREST LAW

OF THE

STATE OF NEW YORK

RELATING TO

GAME, FISH AND WILD ANIMALS, AND TO THE
FOREST PRESERVE AND ADIRON-
DACK PARK.

As Revised and Enacted by the Legislature of 1892 and Amended
by the Legislatures of 1895, 1896, 1897, 1898 and 1899.

WYNKOOP HALLENBECK CRAWFORD CO,
STATE PRINTERS
NEW YORK AND ALBANY
1899

The first snowmobile appeared on the lakes in 1939. In January 2005, members of the Nick Stoner Trailers Snowmobile Club took a break at Vrooman's hotel at Caroga Lake. The club began in 1974 to promote local snowmobiling and improve the trail system in the area. The trails through the lake area are part of the statewide interconnecting snowmobile trail system. On November 30, 2008, emergency crews responded to a call to perform an ice rescue at Pine Lake for two snowmobiles that went through the ice. Although the lake had iced over, the ice was not thick enough to support the weight of both a sled and its rider. Just days earlier, the Caroga Volunteer Fire Department learned they were to receive grant money from US Homeland Security to assist with ice rescues. (Courtesy of the *Leader-Herald*.)

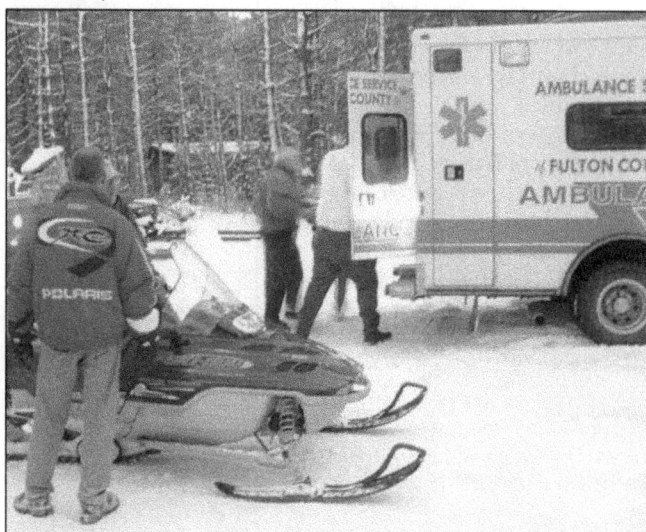

Nine

TRANSPORTATION

It was not always easy to get to the lakes. Although direct train service was proposed, it never developed. Some travelers arrived by coach. Others traveled by steamer. A few dropped out of the air on seaplanes. Some used their own power of locomotion to hike into the lake area. With industry came improved roads. The first paved roads in the area appeared around 1905, replacing the old plank roads. (Courtesy of the Town of Caroga.)

How to Get Here

OUR nearest railway station is Gloversville. Every train on the New York Central, which stops at Fonda, is met by a train of the Fonda, Johnstown & Gloversville Railroad—either steam or electric, or both. The cities of Gloversville and Schenectady are connected by the finest equipped trolley line in the United States, cars leaving either city every thirty minutes. At Gloversville, stages run every day, and livery conveniences can be obtained at very reasonable rates. Distance from Gloversville, twelve miles—a ride of two hours through a beautiful country picturesque with nature's adornment.

For further information address

FRANK MORRIS, MGR.,
Auskerada, Fulton Co., N. Y.

Steamers transported residents and guests from Stewart's Landing to camps around Canada Lake. As the steamer reached capacity, rowboats were strung behind the steamer. Known as "Fulton's Folly," this boat is the *Kanaughta*, built by James Y. Fulton in the early 1890s. The Native American word *Kanata* means "amber-colored water." Over the years, the Fulton County Skin Divers Association members searched the bottom of Canada Lake for steamer remains. (Courtesy of the Town of Caroga.)

Boats served as touring vessels each afternoon on Canada Lake. Some of the steamers were wood fired and left a trail of smoke in their wake. Others, like the *Clermont*, ran on naptha, a flammable liquid. Capt. Louis Ballou was one of the steamer captains who worked the steamboats during the summer months. (Courtesy of the Town of Caroga.)

A few of the steamboats, such as the *Whip-poor-will* shown here, had multiple responsibilities. In addition to transporting people and property around the lake, the power of their steam engines was used to saw wood. On two known occasions, the *Kanaughta* steamer was called upon to assist in search and rescue operations on the lake. (Courtesy of Fulton County Museum.)

Young couples would often rent rowboats to go "look for water lilies." In 1903, one duo rowed out but did not return. George H. Evans, days away from receiving a substantial inheritance from his father's estate, and Florence Brown went missing. Rescue parties searched for two weeks, amidst speculated sightings of them in neighboring towns. After dynamiting a muddy section of Canada Lake, their bodies eventually surfaced and were recovered. (Courtesy of Caroga Historical Association and Museum.)

Although it operated for only two seasons in 1910 and 1911, the Gloversville Auto Stage Company carried guests from the cities of Gloversville and Johnstown northwest to the lake area. The autos were replaced by enclosed and more comfortable Federal buses operated by the Gloversville, Caroga, and Canada Lake Stage Company. (Courtesy of the Town of Caroga.)

Although the cart itself was not uncommon in the lake area, the four-legged team members and its driver are unusual. Shown here is a team of mill-owned oxen being driven by Leander Brush (right), a Native American, around 1900. Oxen were used around the mills to tow log booms, which collected and guided logs across the water toward the sawmill. (Courtesy of the Town of Caroga.)

116

Visitors flocked to Caroga Lake and surrounding communities by the wagon-full at the turn of the 20th century. Sometimes, these wagons would circle camps along the lake, and guests would enjoy (and try to decipher) the names of the camps they passed. Shadyside, Camp WYL, Silver Springs, and Churchill's Landing were just a few of the camps located here. (Courtesy of the Town of Caroga.)

Around 1900, it would take four or more hours to travel from Gloversville to Canada Lake by way of the Canada Lake Horse Stage. The stages traveled on dirt, gravel, or plank roads. Travel changed in 1909, when the Gloversville Auto Stage Company carried up to 10 passengers at a time up to the lakes over macadam roads, reducing the trip to two hours, or less, for $1.25. (Courtesy of David and Catherine Graves.)

Resting on the shore of Green Lake is an Adirondack Guide Boat. Neither a canoe nor a rowboat, the guide boat was developed in the early 1800s to carry a guide and his hunting and camping gear as he traveled about the Adirondack region. Guide boats were used in the lake region by both guides and recreational boaters. Camel's Hump is seen in the background. (Courtesy of Barbara Donnelly.)

Phoebe Dwiggins and Don Dwiggins stand before a World War I Jenny, which was landed on August 5, 1922, by Major Haynor in a field that had been developed as part of the Caroga Recreation Park in Wheelerville. Haynor flew the plane too low on takeoff, clipping the top of a tree on Stoner Island in Canada Lake. He was able to land the plane safely. (Courtesy of the Town of Caroga.)

The first "snowmobile" on Canada Lake was Smitty's iceboat, built in 1939 by Dick Smith, a resident of Green Lake. Smith used salvaged parts from a second-hand motorcycle, which he had wrapped unexpectedly around a tree. Other parts—the propeller, cockpit, and skis—he crafted by hand. Unfortunately, during one spring thaw, the ice moved faster than Smith, and the craft sunk to the bottom of the lake. (Courtesy of Douglas and Judith Smith.)

Air kept boaters both afloat and moving in these bubble boats used on Caroga Lake in the 1920s. Bathers could rent the bubble boats at the dock at Sherman's Park. Although Frank Sherman did not build his new bathhouses and dance pavilion until the winter of 1919–1920, summer at Sherman's began in 1919, with an older bathhouse and beach area. (Courtesy of Donald and Erma Hoffman.)

Lined up on the right from tree to tree are bikes, which were available for rent at Sherman's Park back in the late 1930s. Shown also in this photograph is Trixie's circular fenced house. Located at the bottom of the photograph, Frank Sherman can be seen looking back at the camera. Directly behind him is the hit striker game, a popular "muscle" attraction at the park. (Courtesy of Janet Sherman Shepard.)

The automobile was both friend and foe to destination recreation locations, such as Sherman's Park, shown here in the early 1920s. The automobile allowed local city residents to travel to and enjoy a day at one of the lakes. However, it also offered the freedom to go beyond one's backyard and venture to other lakes and vacation destinations. (Courtesy of Donald and Erma Hoffman.)

The artistic Dwiggins family sported the first kicker in the lake area. Phoebe Dwiggins, in her biographical sketch about her family, shared that she and her brother Don would use this boat to travel across Canada Lake to attend Wheelerville Union Free School during the months they were in residency on the lake. Seen here are their parents, Clare Dwiggins and Betsy Lindsay. (Courtesy of Dona Dise.)

Spring road flooding often accompanied heavy winter snow melt-offs, making travel throughout the lake area challenging, especially on dirt, gravel, or plank roads. The road along Caroga Creek was paved in 1905. The road from Newkirks Mills to Auskerada was paved in 1912. The road from Gloversville would remain a plank road until 1915. In 1926, the road from Green Lake to Stoner Lake was made concrete. (Courtesy of David and Catherine Graves.)

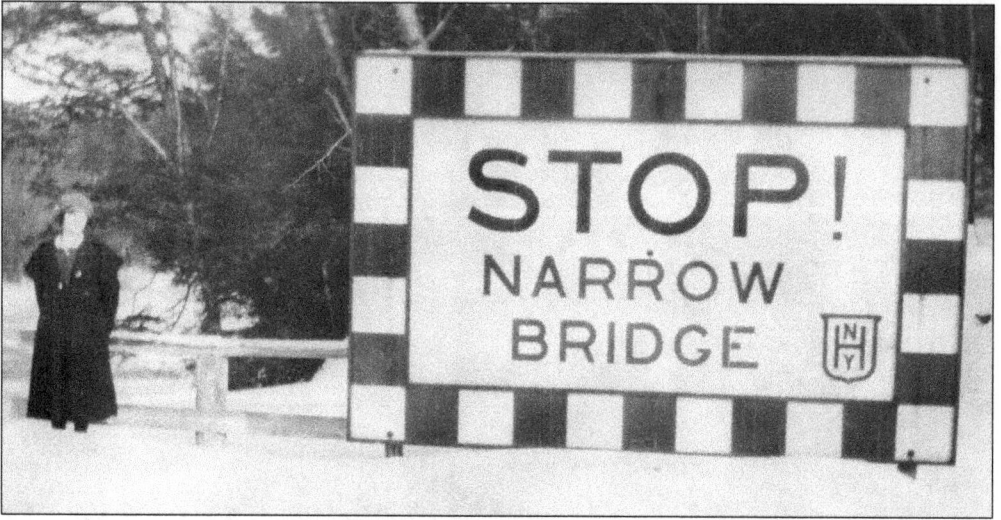

Before Route 10A was constructed, traffic coming from the Johnstown area used Cape Horn Road, which at times was difficult to travel. Florence Kennicult is standing beside a New York Highway Department sign on the lower iron bridge. Peck Creek is in the background. A popular watering trough was at the intersection of Beech Ridge and Cape Horn Road. Residents still stop at this spring today to fill water bottles. (Courtesy of the Town of Caroga.)

Perhaps the greatest engineering feat of the lake area was the rerouting and construction of the state highway in 1940–1941 due to traffic jams on the original road. Apparently, the stopped traffic prevented some uncomfortable residents from reaching their outhouses on the other side of the highway. Rock from Green Mountain had to be blasted away with such force that some of the rock landed in Canada Lake. (Courtesy of David and Catherine Graves.)

This biplane, owned by the Knox Gelatin family, was a frequent visitor on West Caroga Lake in the late 1950s. Seaplanes traveled throughout the Adirondacks, transporting passengers to lakes. In the background is the diving platform, a popular attraction near Sherman's Park. When the beach area would first open each summer, swimmers would have to navigate cold water to reach the platform. During some spring thaws, ice would remain on the lakes until May. (Courtesy of Robert Fear.)

Businesses from the three-lake region participated in the 1976 bicentennial parade in Gloversville. Pine Lake Amusement Park sported a 1924 Sanford fire truck as its entry. Note that the signage on the truck shows Pine Lake Fire Department. The Town of Caroga would establish its fire department in 1951. A building to house the town's fire equipment was constructed in 1953, in part by resident brick donations, costing 25¢ each. (Courtesy of the Town of Caroga.)

A popular ride in the 1960s at Pine Lake Amusement Park was the Custer Cars, which circled some of the cottages. The Custer Cars were moved to Pine Lake from Sherman's Park, which became the home of the Midget Racers, as shown below. After hours, Frank Sherman would permit motorcyclists to ride on the Midget Racer track. The Custer Park Car was created around 1925 by the Custer Specialty Company in Dayton, Ohio. The electric car could run on any surface, which attracted amusement park owners. Because of the opposite locations of the two parks, Sherman's Park attracted families residing east of the lakes in Johnstown and Gloversville. Pine Lake Park drew crowds from the west from Dolgeville, Little Falls, and Herkimer. (Above, courtesy of Wayne and Nancy Seeley; below, courtesy of Donald and Erma Hoffman.)

In the 1980s, campers at Pine Lake Park were treated to horse-drawn wagon rides through the campground. Driving the team of Percherons is Hector "Butch" Miner, being assisted by FritzAnn Surace, who would later become the town supervisor in 1994. Surace would be instrumental in the closing of the town's landfill, as required by the State of New York. (Courtesy of William and Chardel Houck.)

The MDA Run for the Muscular Dystrophy Association on July 15, 1990, was led by Caroga Lake resident Joseph Ricciardi in his 1949 Ford, custom built by George Barris, who is known as the "King of Kustomizers." Barris's designs include cars for *The Munsters* and *The Beverly Hillbillies*. Hundreds of motorcycles toured the surrounding area before heading to Caroga Lake. The MDA Run came to Caroga Lake five times. (Courtesy of Joseph Ricciardi.)

In Barbara McMartin's book, *Fun on Flatwater: An Introduction to Adirondack Canoeing*, one of the kayak trips McMartin spotlighted was a round-trip adventure that started at the outlet of Canada Lake, went to Stewart's Dam, and then returned to Canada Lake. The 10-mile journey took about five hours. McMartin once remarked that this stretch of water was one of the best-kept secrets of the Adirondacks. The flat-water paddle trip traced the old steamer route of days past. McMartin was the author of 25 books, many of which spotlighted the Caroga Lake area. In her book *50 Hikes in the Adirondacks: Short Walks, Day Trips, and Backpacks Throughout the Park*, she guided day-hikers to Good Luck Cliffs, north of Pine Lake. In *Adventures in Hiking: A Young Peoples' Guide to the Adirondacks*, McMartin ventured into Willie Marsh, a wetlands area with rustic boardwalks east of Caroga Lake. And *Hides, Hemlocks, and Adirondack History: How the Tanning Industry Influenced the Region's Growth* included photographs and history of the Wheeler-Claflin Tannery at the inlet to Canada Lake. (Courtesy of Jeannine Schwartz.)

Frank Sherman designed and built a miniature car, fire pumper, snowblower, and mechanical monkeys to help stir popcorn as it popped. In 2006, the *Leader-Herald* showcased Anthony Ermie, as he drove his electric "car of the future" around Caroga Lake on the old Sherman Park grounds. In addition to summering at Pine Lake, Ermie is the creator of CarogaTimes.com, a website spotlighting the history of Caroga Lake and surrounding areas. (Courtesy of the *Leader-Herald*.)

As visitors left the Caroga Lake area and the Adirondack Park in 1975, they were invited to return another day to make more Adirondack memories. The sign shown in this photograph was later replaced by an official Adirondack Park Agency sign, which shows the "Blue Line boundary" of the six million-acre wilderness park. (Courtesy of the Town of Caroga.)

Visit us at
arcadiapublishing.com